Keeping Sabr

Heal with Proven Sunnah Practices
for Emotional Wellbeing and
Mental Strength

SARAH GULFRAZ

Copyright © 2024 Sarah Gulfraz

Sarah Gulfraz has asserted her right to be identified as the author of this Work in accordance with the Copyright, Designs and Patents Act 1988.

All rights reserved.

No portion of this book may be reproduced in any form, stored in a retrieval system, stored in a database, or published/transmitted in any form or by any means, electronic, mechanical, photocopying, recording or otherwise, without prior written permission of the publisher.

Dedication

~ Bismillah ~

May Allah (swt) accept our efforts and grant us success in this life and the next. Ameen.

In dedication to my loving family and all their support.

Contents

1. Introduction — 1
2. Introduction to Islam and Mental Health — 3
3. Sunnah Approach to Emotional Wellness — 21
4. Coping with Anxiety and Stress — 34
5. Overcoming Depression and Sadness — 45
6. Seeking Spiritual Healing — 56
7. Building Resilience and Inner Strength — 67
8. Strengthening Family and Community Support — 86
9. Addressing Trauma and Grief — 98
10. Balancing Mental Health and Spiritual Growth — 108
11. Seeking Professional Help and Guidance — 115
12. Conclusion — 121

Find Out More — 122

Chapter One

Introduction

An integral part of holistic well-being is emotional and mental health. They impact how you view relationships, life, and even your health. When your mental health is strong, you can handle a wide range of emotions connected to different aspects of your life and maintain your control even when things don't go your way.

A person with good mental health can reach their full potential, manage stress in healthy ways, be more productive and draw deeper meaning from their experiences in life. As Muslims, we can benefit from the teachings of Islam that provide us with several options for managing our mental health in a better way.

Islam views mental wellness as a gift from Allah (SWT) or an Amanah. Everybody has an obligation to educate themselves on the subject of mental health because mental health affects not only how we feel, think, and behave but also how we manage stress, interact with others, and make decisions.

Everyone who faces hardships in life occasionally slips into depressive and painful states. Some people experience these emotions for longer than others, and they can occasionally lead to severe depression. Experiencing the comfort of an All-Wise, benevolent Allah (SWT) who knows how to soothe suffering after adversity might help promote healing.

Therefore, a great deal of the Quran and Hadith (narratives about the words, deeds, and character of the Prophet (PBUH)) deal with mental health and well-being issues and provide advice that we should implement in our daily lives.

The Quran's teachings, which offer a spiritual haven and hope for a better future, can lessen suffering. Reading the Quran and remembering Allah (SWT) can lessen negative mental states and emotions, calming the body, mind, and soul.

Since Allah (SWT) is ultimately the one who can heal depression, finding inspiration in the stories in the Quran can, in fact, make the process easier. Furthermore, effective lessons from the life of Prophet Muhammad (PBUH) are also highlighted in this book as examples of how he recognised the value of mental health.

This book examines the relationship between Islam and mental health, offering psychological insights and doable coping mechanisms based on the Sunnah. Every chapter explores a particular facet of resilience, emotional health, and spiritual healing, providing direction to those who want to incorporate Islamic ideas into their mental health journey.

In an era where mental health challenges are increasingly prevalent, this book serves as a valuable resource for anyone seeking to navigate their emotional struggles with the guidance of Islamic teachings. Whether you're dealing with anxiety, depression, trauma, or simply seeking to strengthen your inner resilience, Keeping Sabr offers a compassionate and faith-centred pathway to healing and personal growth.

Let's dive in!

Chapter Two

Introduction to Islam and Mental Health

Understanding mental health in the context of Islamic teachings

Maintaining equilibrium in all facets of your life—social, physical, spiritual, financial, and mental— is called mental health. You might occasionally tip the balance too much in one particular direction, and that's why your mental health gets disturbed. Maintaining your unique personal balance will be your challenge to maintain mental well-being. And finding equilibrium among all these requires nothing special but learning.

Taking care of our mental health is equally as important as taking care of our physical health to maintain strong and healthy bodies. Individuals' mental health can impact their daily lives, interactions, and physical health.

Mental health is a vital aspect of health and well-being that supports our capacity as individuals and as a society to make choices, form bonds with one another, and influence the world around us. Furthermore, it is essential for socioeconomic, communal, and personal growth.

Most people experience anxiety, loneliness, or sadness occasionally because they are human. However, there are moments when people are so depressed, hopeless, anxious, or worthless that they find it difficult to even get out of bed or go anywhere. These emotions may indicate that you require treatment for your mental health. On the other hand, a person with good mental health can manage life's stressors, reach their full potential, learn and work effectively, and give back to their community.

It is important to remember that having good mental health does not guarantee that we will never face stress or be unhappy. However, it does assist us in overcoming them so we may continue living our daily lives productively. It's critical to understand that support is accessible regardless of the biological, life, or family history aspects contributing to mental health issues. To have a better understanding, let's have a look at all its aspects in detail!

What does Islam say about mental health?

According to Islam, a person's capacity to realise their innate spiritual potential is closely tied to their psycho-spiritual well-being. Every human is made to walk a route that will eventually lead to their salvation in the hereafter and their capacity to receive Allah's (SWT) pleasure. Thus, from an Islamic spiritual standpoint, one's capacity to successfully continue on this road of worship indicates one's health.

Therefore, any barriers preventing them from following this path are viewed as harmful to human functioning and deserve attention. This includes obstacles that prevent us from freely worshipping Allah (SWT) on a psychological, bodily, or emotional level. More precisely, as psychological health is a component of total health and well-being, a holistic approach to it needs to be multifaceted.

- Our thoughts: Are they practical, upbeat, and realistic? Are they helping us achieve our daily objectives and tasks?

- Physical well-being includes nutrition and exercise, frequent medical examinations, and cleanliness.

- Spiritual well-being includes fulfilling our required duties to Allah (SWT), such as praying and fasting, and our relationship and connection with Him through Dhikr (remembering Him).

- Social and behavioural health: We have positive, constructive connections and interactions with others. The capacity to acknowledge and resolve disagreement as well as embrace and experience happiness.

- Emotional wellness includes awareness of positive and negative emotions and the capacity to control them in a healthy way.

When these components are balanced and functioning harmoniously, we can achieve optimal mental health. However, mental health is not static; we must consistently and routinely strive to achieve this balance. We are all on a lifelong path to improving our mental, spiritual, psychological, and mature well-being.

This is considered a balance since achieving optimal mental wellness is nonlinear. That being said, if you discover persistently out-of-balance behavioural or emotional habits, you must assess the situation and determine how to resume your efforts to achieve balance.

Mental health issues are caused by a variety of reasons, including:

- Anatomical elements like brain chemistry or genes

- A family history of psychological issues

- Life events like abuse or trauma

According to Islamic teachings, maintaining a balance between one's spirit, mind, and behaviour is necessary for mental health, which is seen as an essential component of general health. The following are some essential elements of the Islamic viewpoint on mental health:

Self-Restraint: Islam instructs people to avoid doing things that hurt themselves or other people and control their selves and passions. It supports the person's emotional and psychological equilibrium.

Faith and Mental Calm: Worshipping Allah (SWT) and having faith are sources of strength and serenity. People are supposed to find peace of mind and grow closer to Allah (SWT) through worshipping, praying, and remembering Him amid life's hardships.

Pardon and Act Righteously: Islam emphasises the value of showing kindness and forgiveness to others. Acts of kindness can lessen social tensions that negatively impact mental health and enhance mental well-being.

Inner Contentment: Islam emphasises the value of endurance and surrendering to Allah's (SWT) will. People who are content with all of His provisions can confront difficult circumstances composedly and honestly face every test of life.

Social Context and Family Assistance: Islam places a strong emphasis on the value of familial and social support in preserving mental health. Mutual assistance is necessary for families and communities to deal with mental health challenges.

Knowledge and Consciousness: Islam urges its adherents to dispel the stigma attached to mental illness and educate themselves and the wider public on the value of mental health. Those who are aware of mental health difficulties are better able to get the support and assistance they need.

The Pursuit of Information: In Islam, knowledge is fundamental. Gaining more understanding about mental health might make it easier for people to recognise and manage psychological issues.

From an Islamic standpoint, mental well-being is an essential component of total health, and it is anticipated that people will retain improved mental health and enhance their general well-being by incorporating Islamic teachings into their everyday lives.

Nobody is ever truly happy. We are especially susceptible to an emotional roller coaster since fundamental brain changes occur throughout our lives. These emotional highs and lows are a natural part of growing up. While mental health issues are widespread, assistance is available. Individuals with mental health issues are capable of improving, and many even fully recover.

Like everyone else, Muslims experience life's hardships and unsettling ideas, but they can handle them considerably better because they have a comprehensive understanding of their origins, destinations, and motivations. This knowledge gives them a significant advantage.

In a crisis, someone who feels lost and alone will likely experience depression and helplessness. But because there is a strong helping hand to grasp while navigating life's challenges, someone who feels supported by a kind Allah (SWT) who loves, hears cries of desperation and gives generous help has a better chance of getting back on track much faster.

We are not required to be superhuman by Islam. We are advised to resist bad emotions by thinking positively and acting accordingly. When this peaceful equilibrium is upset, people experience depression or sadness. In these situations, Islam intervenes—not to condemn the emotion but to provide a means of regaining mental and psychological harmony.

> *As Allah (SWT) says in the Quran: "And for those who fear Allah (SWT), He always prepares a way out, and He provides for him from sources he never could imagine, And if anyone puts his trust in Allah (SWT), sufficient is Allah (SWT) for him, For Allah (SWT) will surely*

accomplish His purpose: verily, for all things has Allah appointed a due proportion." (Quran 65:2-3)

Mental health impacts all areas of life, making it a crucial component of overall well-being. Now, let's examine Islam's stance on mental health, which provides helpful advice and insights derived from verses in the Quran and Hadiths (sayings of the Holy Prophet PBUH).

Quranic perspectives on psychological well-being and spiritual healing

Islam is a flawless, well-organised, and systematic faith. It is a way of life since it teaches Muslims how to live purposeful lives. The excellence of its teachings encompasses many facets of human existence, such as emotional and mental health care. Since the biopsychosocial framework is used to conceptualise mental health and illness, Islam offers a unique viewpoint on these topics and well-being.

Muslims' mental and emotional health is greatly influenced by the Quran, which provides direction, comfort, and a framework for leading a balanced life. Its teachings offer a framework for handling mental health concerns in an Islamic setting.

Although the term "mental health" is not explicitly used in the Quran, Allah (SWT) alludes to the pressures of life in verses like this one, which allude to the stresses we will face in this life:

> *"And we will surely test you with something of fear and hunger and a loss of wealth and lives and crops, but give good tidings to the patient." (Quran 2:155)*

Although this verse helps us emotionally and mentally prepare for the trials and tribulations life will present, it also serves as a reminder that these will be followed by delayed gratification and the confidence that our patience will be rewarded. A significant portion of our identity as Muslims is derived from our faith in Allah (SWT), which must be acknowledged should someone seek out professional mental health care for their own well-being.

Furthermore, by encouraging religion, tolerance, thankfulness, justice, and knowledge-seeking, the Quran supports mental health. It reassures believers that with hardship comes ease (Quran 94:5-6) and that Allah (SWT) does not burden any soul beyond its capacity (Quran 2:286).

These teachings uplift spirituality, impart meaning and hope, and control uncomfortable feelings. The five daily prayers and the remembrance of Allah (SWT) are mental-calming practices. Islam discourages extreme behaviour and encourages self-control, moderation, and balance—all of which are beneficial to mental health.

The Quran contains numerous verses emphasising the value of healthy mental skills.

> *"Do not give the weak-minded your property." (Quran 4:5)*

Along with protecting riches, family, life, and religion, one of the five main goals of Islamic law is the maintenance of mental faculties. Anything that is thought to damage mental abilities, such as alcoholism, is discouraged.

Moreover, it is thought that reading the Quran can improve mental health on a psychological and spiritual level, even if it is not a direct medical remedy for mental health issues. One can find peace of mind by solemnly and quietly reading the Quran. Reading the wise verses in the Quran can also reduce stress and anxiety.

Muslims' mental and emotional health is greatly influenced by the Quran. Its teachings include moral, social, psychological, and spiritual guidance promoting an all-encompassing well-being approach. People who interact with the Quran can discover serenity, resiliency, and a sense of direction that aids them in overcoming obstacles in life.

Importance of addressing mental health challenges within the Muslim community

Having a sound mind is essential to living a happy and fulfilled life. Several social, cultural, and religious elements contribute to the stigma associated with mental health talk among Muslims. Nonetheless, Muslims require mental health help just like everyone else.

Muslims have a wide range of experiences and backgrounds. Everybody faces hardships in life and tries to keep their mental health intact. But to keep things in perspective, we need to know that Islam advises Muslims to have a means of getting mental health services when they need them to address mental health disorders.

It is difficult to address mental health issues in the Muslim community for a number of reasons. There are strong cultural taboos against discussing any personal or family concerns with outsiders; shame and stigma seem to be the biggest barriers to receiving mental health care. Shame is one of the most common challenges.

Additionally, there are the typical difficulties that many young Muslims encounter. Identity conflicts are inevitable when one grows up with values and views that differ from those of the culture in which they are raised.

In addition, the high prevalence of Islamophobia that many Muslims experience, the under-representation of Muslims, and the identity crisis all raise concerns about mental health.

Misinformation and neglect about mental health are caused by a severe lack of knowledge and instruction in the field. People who have cultural or religious beliefs that link mental illness to spiritual origins may be reluctant to seek professional assistance. Language hurdles and the lack of Muslim mental health experts exacerbate the lack of access to culturally acceptable care.

Moreover, access to care is made more difficult by gender-specific issues, financial constraints, and social isolation, which is particularly common among immigrants and refugees. In addition, community resources are frequently lacking, and mental health efforts are frequently underfunded.

Beyond this, however, many Muslim communities are falling behind in terms of attitudes and awareness around mental health. Psychology and counselling are still widely misunderstood and stigmatised; they are perceived as a secular substitute for spiritual healing that is incompatible with religious beliefs. Mental health issues are frequently minimised or written off as a sign of a lack of faith or willpower, and they are rarely given the attention they require to address their complex, deeply ingrained nature.

Many Muslims find it difficult to ask for assistance or have candid conversations regarding these matters. Furthermore, individuals who internalise these stigmas now hold themselves responsible for their struggles because of their lack of faith, which has caused them to struggle.

How does this affect their relationship with their religion and their mental health even more if they keep looking for spiritual guidance but are still having difficulties?

This way of thinking is not at all Islamic. Islam and psychology have a long history, with early Islamic philosophers like Al-Ghazali establishing the groundwork for modern psychology and cognitive behaviour therapy. Muslims are advised to address mental health concerns seriously by Islamic literature.

Islam has long pushed for practical action towards overcoming mental illness and seeking assistance. In fact, current research has demonstrated that combining psychological therapy with spiritual beliefs can be very successful.

Seeing the significance of mental health in all facets of life, it is imperative to safeguard and enhance psychological well-being through proper approaches. Many Muslims suffer from mental illness. As a result, they are more likely to face difficulties in their relationships, physical health problems, and life disruptions.

In the end, poor mental health prevents Muslims from concentrating on preparing for the afterlife. Because of this, Muslims must prioritise their mental health and deal with any problems that may come up. Early intervention for mental health issues has the power to transform and perhaps save lives.

Negative consequences on your life, such as untreated mental diseases, might result from neglecting your mental health. Finding a good balance in your life will depend on keeping your mental health in check and taking care of any mental health issues you may have.

Sadly, the majority of Muslims who experience mental health issues don't get the support they need. Mental health difficulties endure and cause problems for both individuals and society when there is no drive or readiness to seek care or when there is fear of what others may think is impeding progress.

Because of this, it's more crucial than ever that we have honest conversations about mental health and give individuals the confidence or support they need to obtain the care they need. When someone is on the road to recovery and wants to change their course, treatment can be quite important.

If you're unsure about where to begin or with whom to discuss your mental health, keep reading!

Stigma and misconceptions surrounding mental illness

A significant obstacle for those who have a mental illness is still the stigma associated with mental illness. Even if the state of mental health care has greatly improved in recent years, many people still decide not to get treatment or end it too soon.

Stigma is one of the many potential causes of these differences, albeit arguably the most important. Stigma causes inequities and even disastrous outcomes for people with mental illnesses as well as their communities.

People may decide not to associate with mental health clinics or experts to avoid being labelled as psychiatric patients; this way, they can escape being diagnosed by not seeking mental health care.

Discrimination and prejudice that prevents people from obtaining housing, health care, work, or educational opportunities is known as public stigma. When the broader population accepts and behaves based on preconceived notions about mental illness, it is known as public stigma.

Let's look at these misconceptions and how they impact people who are looking for assistance.

Given the stigma associated with mental health issues and the belief that they make one less loyal, many Muslims are reluctant to discuss their problems in public. This prejudice stems from well-ingrained societal norms that erroneously link mental illness to apathy or weakness. Some people may be discouraged from getting treatment for mental health illnesses due to the stigma attached to it.

Cultural restrictions in many Muslim communities might make it difficult for members to discuss issues openly. These barriers to empathy and understanding may make those who are struggling with mental illness feel even more alone.

Many Muslims do not seek therapy for mental health issues because they believe that they are tests from Allah (SWT). Misunderstandings of Islamic doctrines lead some Muslims to attribute mental health issues to a lack of faith or divine vengeance. This misconception brings about more obstacles to mental health therapy.

Last but not least, in many countries with substantial Muslim populations, it's possible that there aren't enough resources or awareness to support Muslim mental health issues, leading to a shortage of trained professionals and easily accessible therapy. People with mental health issues may find it challenging to acquire the care they need because of a lack of resources and a general lack of awareness of these issues.

Muslims are subject to the challenges of life, just like followers of any other religion. They typically handle a distinct set of issues that could be detrimental to Muslim mental health.

Muslims can be empowered to manage the intricacies of their mental health journey by using the teachings of Islam, comprehensive wellness practices, and personalised coaching.

Dispelling myths and promoting awareness of mental health issues

Within the Muslim community, mental health is a taboo subject that is veiled in layers of false information and beliefs. Many times, people deny that mental health issues exist at all or that spirituality might help to improve mental health.

Busting the myths surrounding mental health can help end the stigma and foster a culture that supports individuals of all ages getting the treatment they need. The following are a few widespread myths regarding mental health:

- **Myth 1: Depressive and anxious states stem from low faith (Iman).**

While this remark may have a kernel of truth, it is primarily detrimental and problematic. There is the tale of Hazrat Yaqub (AS), who lost his sight due to his unrelenting and intense grief over the passing of Hazrat Yusuf (AS). This story does teach us that great sorrow is not a symptom of weak Iman, even if it is unlikely that this was depression because Hazrat Yaqub (AS) undoubtedly possessed more Iman than any living person. Rather, it was likely a reaction to grief.

Mental health problems have multiple underlying causes. It is recognised that a person's health is influenced by a complex interplay of bio, psycho, social, and spiritual variables.

Therefore, while an excess of sin, heart hardness, and pessimism towards Allah (SWT) may be risk factors for poor mental health from a spiritual standpoint, there are also a plethora of other biological, psychological, and social elements that might put an individual in danger.

Psychological variables such as negative thinking and low self-esteem are well-known. Some recognised biological causes include low serotonin levels, hereditary predisposition, and childbirth. In a similar vein, social risk factors encompass situations like poverty, marginalisation, isolation, and refugee status.

We run the risk of exacerbating someone's condition and increasing their sense of hopelessness when we assign blame, saying that their mental illness is a symptom of poor iman. Since mental health problems can arise from a variety of factors, it is unfair to oversimplify complex medical conditions in this way, as it ignores the possible assistance that mental health specialists may be able to provide.

The main point is that, as Muslims, we shouldn't generalise about everyone and make judgemental remarks. Rather, we ought to make insightful and sympathetic remarks.

- **Myth 2: Allah (SWT) is punishing you, which is why you are depressed.**

This argument's premise is that you have no cause to be depressed if you have faith and hope in Allah (SWT). By that reasoning, devout Muslims would never develop diabetes since, in accordance with the Holy Prophet's (PBUH) Hadith, we would fast on Mondays and Thursdays and only eat till we reached the third part of our stomach. One could get type I diabetes even then.

However, as we are all aware, most of us fall short of these ideal norms. However, does that mean we are terrible Muslims? It's what gives us our humanity. Therefore, in the same spirit, condemning those who suffer from mental health issues is an indication of our ignorance.

Mental health issues must now be treated like any other illness. It resembles a test from Allah (SWT), through which He will, hopefully, pardon our transgressions and raise our status.

Never, according to the Holy Prophet (PBUH), does a believer experience pain, adversity, illness, sadness, or even mental anxiety that his sins are not atoned for. Individuals who battle mental health issues emerge from them stronger and with profound insights that others may not have.

- **Myth 3: Depression is all in your mind.**

This is an extremely disrespectful comment that attempts to discredit the experiences of people who struggle with mental health problems. In fact, it is well acknowledged that the pathophysiology of mental diseases involves neurotransmitter dysfunction, with an excess of negative thoughts serving as a common psychological reason.

However, the impacts of mental health conditions like depression extend beyond the skull. The mind, like any other part of the body, can become unwell, and this is the case with mental diseases. Therefore, depression is not solely in the mind.

- **Myth 4: Why can't I visit an imam directly? Why do I need to seek a medical professional?**

As was already said, there are numerous aspects to mental health disorders. Imams are typically highly knowledgeable and skilled in handling spiritual issues. Nonetheless, the majority of imams lack first aid or mental health training. There might be a difference in the knowledge between an imam and a mental health practitioner, even though many Muslims turn to imams for guidance or assistance.

However, it is plausible that certain imams possess such extensive counselling expertise that they are skilled in utilising Islam to provide a form of informal psychotherapy. However, this may not always be the case.

> *Allah (SWT) says in the Quran, "Ask the people of knowledge if you do not know." (Quran 16:43)*

What's required is the creation of a reference system that allows physicians, psychologists, and imams to collaborate and refer one another for diseases that each of their specialities covers.

- **Myth 5: Your mental health issues can be resolved by just reciting the Quran more often and praying more.**

To address this misperception, let's apply the diabetes analogy. Why not recite the Quran and pray instead of taking medicine and working out? The Holy Prophet (PBUH) taught us to use medications to treat our diseases. He instructed us to exercise caution and have faith in Allah (SWT). Then, of course, we can employ the Quran as a treatment and offer prayers for Shifa.

It is true, nonetheless, that the Quran has a profoundly positive impact on mental health. As Allah (SWT) states, the Quran is shifa, or healing, for what is in the hearts. But reading it thoughtfully and with comprehension yields the greatest usefulness. The Quran accomplishes this by instilling hope and changing our way of thinking to a more constructive one.

Dispelling these myths is considered necessary because Islam emphasises the importance of safeguarding one's bodily, mental, and even spiritual well-being. Although we must deepen our relationship with Allah (SWT), we nonetheless seek professional assistance when faced with challenging circumstances. We must take care of and preserve this body, which the Almighty has given us.

Furthermore, raising awareness of mental health issues is a crucial societal movement that will help to expand access to care and foster better understanding. By sharing our own experiences, we may work to lessen the stigma associated with mental illness and mental health issues. This is known as mental health awareness.

The underappreciation of mental health is a global problem that affects Muslim populations far more than just them. For those who comprehend, it is each of our responsibilities to teach people in our communities and families as well as those around us. To completely eradicate these stigmas, we must all contribute to bringing these conversations to the forefront of our communities and tackling them one step at a time. Increasing knowledge of mental health issues can benefit you in understanding mental illness and its symptoms as well as others around you, particularly your friends and family who may be affected.

Encouraging compassion and support for individuals struggling with mental health

Having compassion entails treating everyone with respect and caring for them. In the context of treating mental illness, compassion is having an awareness of the mental and emotional suffering of others. It all comes down to being kind to others, being aware of their difficulties, and sincerely trying to help them feel better. This goes beyond simply applying medication and therapeutic techniques; it also involves acknowledging that each person seeking assistance is unique with sentiments of their own.

This approach's superpowers are mental health care support and compassion. Individuals who experience emotional support and validation are more inclined to engage in their wellness initiatives fully. People find it simpler to take control of their well-being when compassionate, whether changing their lifestyle, taking medication, or attending therapy.

Being compassionate is more than simply a feel-good emotion; it may act as a motivator to maintain your wellness goals. When you have a genuine relationship with your healthcare friends, you are more likely to follow their advice. This includes taking your medication as prescribed, attending treatment like a pro, and engaging in positive activities that will make you happier and healthier overall.

Consider visiting a location where you are treated more like a person than a patient. In mental health care, compassion does just that—it elevates the encounter to a unique level. When you feel deeply heard and seen, trust is formed between you and your healthcare staff. This trust is the key to having better conversations, working as a team, and opening up about your mental health journey.

Being compassionate is for the entire group, not just for one individual! It's like making a cosy nest when mental health professionals foster a compassionate atmosphere. Everyone is encouraged by this nest to feel comfortable asking for assistance without fear of criticism.

A community can become a place where everyone feels welcome by dispelling outdated notions about mental health and embracing empathy. In sum, compassion and support are the keys to a happy and healthier journey with mental health.

Strategies for compassionate support for Muslims struggling with mental health involve understanding and respecting their unique cultural and religious contexts. Mental health professionals should undergo cultural competency training to grasp Islamic beliefs and practices.

Integrating faith-based practices, such as prayer and religious texts, into therapy can enhance trust and effectiveness. Creating safe, stigma-free environments encourages openness and acceptance. Collaboration with religious leaders can bridge the gap between faith and mental health care.

Providing resources in native languages and promoting mental health education within the community also ensures accessibility and awareness, fostering a supportive environment for mental wellness.

> *Allah (SWT) says in the Quran, "And we have certainly created man, and we know what his soul whispers to him, and we are closer to him than [his] jugular vein." (Quran 50:16)*

This verse emphasises the closeness and understanding of Allah (SWT) towards every individual, which can be comforting and supportive for Muslims dealing with mental health issues. Integrating such faith-based elements into mental health care can help Muslims build trust and effectiveness.

Chapter Three

Sunnah Approach to Emotional Wellness

Prophetic guidance on managing emotions and inner struggles

Prophetic guidance emphasises the importance of mental health, recognising the holistic well-being of individuals, encompassing both physical and mental aspects. The Holy Prophet (PBUH) presented himself as a role model for Muslims in every aspect of life, including mental health concerns.

> *Allah (SWT) says: Indeed, in the Messenger of Allah (SWT), you have an excellent example for whoever has hope in Allah (SWT) and the Last Day and remembers Allah (SWT) often. (Quran 33:21)*

The Prophetic tradition offers a comprehensive foundation for fostering mental health. The Holy Prophet (PBUH) promoted healthy habits and cleanliness, including eating a balanced diet, getting enough sleep, and exercising. He forbade practices like drinking and drug misuse, which are today recognised to have a detrimental effect on mental health. His lessons were intended to reduce suffering. Prophet Muhammad (PBUH) emphasises the connection between physical and mental health in several Hadiths.

The Prophet Muhammad (PBUH) made the following dua, acknowledging the legitimacy of psychological anguish and the necessity of treatment.

> *The Prophet Muhammad (PBUH) said, "No fatigue, illness, sorrow, sadness, pain, or distress afflicts a Muslim, even if it is as small as the prick of a thorn, except that Allah (SWT) forgives some of their sins because of it." (Sahih Bukhari)*

This demonstrates the Prophet's (PBUH) comprehension of people's mental and emotional challenges. His prayer suggests that he knew these challenges and went to Allah (SWT) for help. At the same time, obtaining professional aid and receiving medical and professional support for health disorders, including mental health challenges, is advised in Islam.

> *The Prophet (PBUH) urged people to get medical attention. He (PBUH) said, "Seek medical treatment, for Allah (SWT) has created a remedy for every disease except one—old age." (Sunah Abu Dawood)*

> *He (PBUH) also stated that: "Allah (SWT) has sent down the disease and the cure, and He has provided a remedy for every illness. Therefore, seek treatment." (Sunah Abu Dawood)*

Hence, the Prophet (PBUH) counsels us to employ medical care and get the proper assistance. He (PBUH) not only urged us to confront and resolve our mental health problems head-on, but he also established the framework that other Islamic scholars used to identify, treat, and support mental health conditions.

We also learnt from the Prophet (PBUH) how important it is to accept and acknowledge our feelings. According to the Prophet Muhammad (PBUH), true strength is the ability to manage anger and maintain composure in the face of difficulty. In times of emotional upheaval, he counselled finding solace in Allah (SWT) and cultivating thankfulness to keep a balanced viewpoint.

People can overcome their inner troubles and develop inner serenity and resilience by reflecting on the transient nature of life's obstacles, acting kindly towards others, and keeping a close relationship with Allah (SWT) via frequent prayer and remembering.

Examples of emotional resilience and psychological coping strategies from the Sunnah

There are many obstacles and problems in life. We Muslims believe that there will be tests for us in this world. Any adversity is unavoidable, but how we handle it shows what kind of person we are. In positive psychology, one of the adaptive coping strategies to deal with crisis is psychological resilience. Resilience is a key factor in protecting and promoting good mental health.

It can serve as a buffer against psychological suffering in unfavourable circumstances like trauma or loss and support the control of stress and symptoms associated with depression. Muslims who possess greater resilience are less likely to suffer from mental health issues.

Stress can eventually hurt our physical, mental, and emotional health. Muslims who possess psychological resilience are better able to fend off its effects and restore control over their life. They are resilient, so they can easily move backwards on the mental health continuum and towards mental wellness. Therefore, building resilience could be a highly powerful, all-encompassing approach to preventing mental health disorders.

Anxiety and despair are just two more major mental health issues that resilience can help shield you from. If you develop better coping mechanisms, you'll become stronger, happier, and more equipped to handle the difficulties you encounter in life, at work, and in your relationships.

Now let's have a look at proven ways to manage our mental health in the light of the Holy Prophet (PBUH) Sunnah:

Negative psychological conditions and emotions are mitigated by reciting the Quran and recalling Allah (SWT), which has a soothing impact on the body, mind, and soul. Since Allah (SWT) is ultimately the one who can heal depression, finding inspiration in the stories found in the Quran can, in fact, make the process easier.

Nevertheless, consulting a specialist is crucial. Consequently, the importance of the Quran in combating depressive disorders shouldn't deter someone from getting help from a licensed therapist when necessary.

> *The Prophet Muhammad (PBUH) said, "Verily, in the remembrance of Allah (SWT) do hearts find rest." (Sahih Muslim)*

This Hadith highlights the calming and soothing effects of remembering Allah (SWT), which can help alleviate emotional and psychological distress.

Tips for Mental Health from Sunnah

For the sake of the Muslim Ummah, the Holy Prophet (PBUH) recognised and addressed psychological issues. In their lifetimes, almost all prophets went through periods of sadness, anxiety, and grief.

The Holy Prophet (PBUH) was so overcome with sadness following the deaths of his cherished wife, Khadijah (RA), and his uncle Abu Talib, as well as the economic and social boycott of Muslims in Makkah. As the Prophet's (PBUH) health began to worsen, Allah (SWT) revealed the following ayah to him due to his worry for people in Makkah who rejected Islam:

> "Perhaps, you would kill yourself (O Muhammad PBUH) in grief, over their footsteps (for their turning away from you), because they believe not in this narration (the Quran)." (Quran 18:6)

Men with understanding can gain infinite wisdom from the Quran and the Sunnah. There is a lot to learn, regardless of your religion or group. Remind yourself that ease follows adversity if you feel hopeless and anxious. Allah (SWT) has stated:

> "For indeed, with hardship ease. Indeed, with hardship ease." (Quran 94:5-6)

Additionally, live in the now and pay attention to the Hereafter. Many of us let our worries about the future and unresolved regrets from our past hold us back. Concentrating on being in the now may improve one's mental health.

> *It is narrated by Abdullah ibn Abbas (RA) that the Holy Prophet (PBUH) said, "Be mindful of Allah (SWT), and you will find Him in front of you. Recognise and acknowledge Allah in times of ease and prosperity, and He will remember you in times of adversity. And know that what has passed you by was not going to befall you, and what has befallen you was not going to pass you by. And know that victory comes with patience, relief with affliction, and hardship with ease." (Tirmidhi)*

The above Hadith, which advises not to worry over what has happened to you or what has not come to pass, is full of wisdom.

When it comes to a person's mental health, the mind seems to have the biggest influence, but many people are unaware of how mindfulness might improve psychological well-being. When practising mindfulness, one embraces feelings and experiences and keeps their attention on the here and now.

Throughout his life, the Prophet Muhammad (PBUH) frequently engaged in mindfulness exercises through self-reflection, prayer, meditation, and remembering Allah (SWT).

> *He (PBUH) said: "It is that you should serve Allah (SWT) as though you could see Him, for though you cannot see Him yet He sees you." (Sahih Bukhari)*

In the story above, attention leads to the refinement and attractiveness of our consciousness of Allah (God). This is so we can develop a closer relationship and feel more at peace with Allah when we concentrate on the here and now.

Integrating these activities into our everyday routines can establish a robust basis for our psychological and emotional welfare. It's critical to keep in mind that getting expert assistance is necessary and does not indicate weakness. It's our duty as Muslims to prioritise maintaining our mental and physical well-being.

Lessons on patience, gratitude, and reliance on Allah (Tawakkul) in times of distress

We frequently encounter difficult situations that test our fortitude, endurance, and faith. Many of us go to the Quran and Sunnah for consolation and guidance when faced with adversity, as they provide us with strength and solace.

Islam gives us an outlook that sees this world as a temporary home, where Allah (SWT) tests His people solely to strengthen their faith when it falters, atone for their transgressions, and bring out the best in each of them. It is advised that Muslims should use resources from the vast array of Islamic teachings and the life of the Holy Prophet (PBUH) to persevere through hardship with thankfulness, patience, and faith in Allah (SWT).

First and foremost, Islam counsels patience in all circumstances. However, guidance and teachings alone are insufficient when one is going through a difficult moment and has a heavy heart. Because of this, Islam offers us the Holy Prophet (PBUH) as a role model. We can read his life like it's a book. Read about the Holy Prophet's (PBUH) patience when facing hardships and needing patience.

When the Holy Prophet (PBUH) proclaimed himself a prophet of Allah (SWT) and invited polytheists to follow Allah (SWT), he experienced numerous tragedies; however, the Holy Prophet (PBUH) showed the greatest amount of patience in the face of every adversity.

For this reason, we look forward to the Holy Prophet (PBUH) as an example of patience and perseverance. He is unmatched in his steadfastness. We ought to take inspiration from the life of the Prophet

Muhammad (PBUH) and endeavour to exhibit the same patience that he possessed.

> *The Prophet (PBUH) emphasised the importance of patience during hardships, as reflected in his saying, "If he is harmed, then he shows patience, and thus there is good for him." (Sahih Muslim)*

Patience helps build resilience, allowing individuals to cope with stress and adversity without succumbing to despair. This resilience is crucial for maintaining mental health in challenging times.

Moreover, cultivating thankfulness is a powerful protective element that supports mental wellness. Gratitude has a gradual effect, but if someone counts their blessings on a regular basis, the benefits are long-lasting and extremely fulfilling. Being thankful will calm the mind and help to relieve stress and anxiety when handling difficult circumstances.

The Prophet Muhammad (PBUH) urged his adherents to express gratitude for life's blessings. Gratitude notebooks are a great tool for recognising the things we should be grateful for in our lives. By cultivating contentment and thankfulness, one can refocus their attention from what they lack to what they have, which enhances their mental health.

Last but not least, having faith in Allah (SWT) reduces tension and worry and gives courage when faced with difficulties. Giving your troubles to Allah (SWT) helps you think positively. Tawakkul can be included in daily living to improve mental wellness. Tawakkul promotes resilience and inner serenity in mental health.

Allah (SWT) is Al-Wakeel, the one in charge of and provides for the needs of His worshippers. He never deserts them or turns them over to anyone else. We know this is a fundamental quality of His since He has revealed this Name to us and given it to Himself; hence, we shall never be disappointed. We are confident that Allah (SWT) will provide us with something better, even if things do not turn out as planned. No one we could have trusted more with our business than Him. For this reason, whenever the Quran mentions depending on Allah (SWT), he serves as a reminder of His omnipotence:

> *"[He is] the Lord of the East and the West; there is no deity except Him, so take Him as Disposer of [your] affairs." (Quran 73:9)*

The Prophet Muhammad (PBUH) exemplified Tawakkul throughout his life, especially during the trials of Makkah and the migration to Medina. Despite facing immense challenges, he remained steadfast, knowing Allah (SWT) was his protector and guide.

Tawakkul, or reliance upon Allah (SWT), is not merely a theological concept but a practical tool that significantly impacts mental health. By reducing anxiety, enhancing resilience, promoting inner peace, and fostering a positive outlook, Tawakkul offers a pathway to mental well-being. Through prayer, reflection, gratitude, and seeking knowledge, one can cultivate and strengthen this reliance, finding solace in the belief that Allah's (SWT) wisdom and support are ever-present.

Getting inspired by the prophets' stories

Strong lessons can be learned from the Prophets' (PBUH) inspiring tales of tenacity. Thinking back on their enormous struggles and unflinching patience can inspire us to be resilient ourselves.

Prophet Muhammad (PBUH) suffered the tragic loss of his beloved wife, Khadija (RA), who stood by him in the face of persecution. He was mistreated and rejected because he spoke the truth. Despite his anguish, suffering, and challenges, he maintained his composure and faith in completing his task.

Prophet Yusuf (AS) endured years of trauma, betrayal, and incarceration. But he persisted in believing that Allah (SWT) was the source of his strength.

> He advises: "No one despairs of relief from Allah (SWT) except the disbelieving people." (Quran 12:87)

Prophet Ayyub (AS) lost everything, including his fortune, family, belongings, and health. He suffered from severe sickness and was left penniless.

> He turned to Allah (SWT) and said, "Truly distress has seized me but You are the Most Merciful of those who are merciful" (Quran 21:83)

The accounts of the Prophets demonstrate how seeking refuge in Allah (SWT) bestows upon us the forbearance and tenacity necessary to triumph over the most formidable challenges. Making the connection between their experiences and our own struggles gives us insight and discernment into keeping our confidence in the Most Merciful during our trials.

Recognising the spiritual dimensions of mental health

Many people turn to spirituality as a deep well at challenging moments. It strengthens inner serenity and gives us a feeling of unity with something bigger than ourselves. When approached with deliberate practice, spirituality can help improve mental health.

KEEPING SABR

The three facets of Islam are law, theology, and spirituality, or Islam, Iman, and Ihsan. Put differently, it may be argued that faith, submission, and spiritual perfection serve as the cornerstones of Islam.

The initial aspect is founded on the five fundamental pillars of Islamic ritual and practice, which include the all-encompassing faith and reverence for Allah (SWT) and his Messenger Muhammad (PBUH), five daily prayers performed in a specific manner and at specific times, fasting throughout Ramadan, donating over two per cent of one's wealth to charitable causes, and a once-in-a-lifetime journey to Makkah.

These pillars address how the human body is controlled.

> *Narrated Ibn Umar: The Holy Prophet (PBUH) said: "Islam is based on (the following) five (principles): 1. To testify that none has the right to be worshipped but Allah (SWT) and Muhammad is Allah's (SWT) Messenger (PBUH). 2. To offer the (compulsory congregational) prayers dutifully and perfectly. 3. To pay Zakat (i.e. obligatory charity). 4. To perform Hajj (i.e. Pilgrimage to Makkah). 5. To observe fast during the month of Ramadan." (Sahih Bukhari)*

The mind is governed by the second dimension, Iman, which also provides the six main beliefs of destiny, divine texts, angels, the Day of Judgement, and the one true God, Allah (SWT), as well as his messengers and prophets. This component outlines the mindset of a sincere follower of Islam.

> *Allah (SWT) states in the Quran, "O you who have believed, believe in Allah (SWT) and His Messenger and the Book that He sent down upon His Messenger and*

the Scripture which He sent down before. And whoever disbelieves in Allah (SWT), His angels, His books, His messengers, and the Last Day has certainly gone far astray." (Quran 4:136)

Lastly, the perfection of faith is the subject of the third dimension, Ihsan. It is fundamental to Islamic spirituality to worship Allah (SWT) as though one sees him, or even if one does not, one should worship in such a way as to imply that Allah (SWT) is watching over each and every person and is aware of every action and thought.

The only way to achieve it is to "adorn the soul with meritorious attributes such as endurance, reliance on Allah (SWT), truthfulness, and love of Allah (SWT) and purify the soul of base traits such as deception, envy, pride, and arrogance."

Ihsan, or Islamic spirituality, is very important since it is the path to both internal and exterior harmony and peace. A person can have inner peace when they are at peace with their body, mind, and spirit. In extrinsic harmony, everyone is gathered around the believer, emphasising understanding and support for one another.

Muslims can find serenity in eternity and life because they believe in the everlasting soul and life after death. Islamic spirituality makes this possible. It is also noteworthy because it encourages people to accept life as it is, with all its trials and injustices and beautiful and joyful moments, by teaching them to have faith in Allah (SWT) and fate.

Recognising the spiritual dimensions of mental health through the lens of Islam provides a robust framework for inner peace and resilience.

Integrating law, theology, and spirituality in daily life can significantly enhance mental well-being, offering a path to cope with life's challenges and find lasting serenity.

Therapeutic Approaches for Enhancing Spiritual and Mental Well-being

In Islamic therapeutic treatments, the following procedures must be carried out by professionals with the necessary training. These interventions are too big for one person to handle alone. By giving the details, the bottom-up approach aims to illustrate the comprehensive aspect of wellness and healing.

In Islam, transformation involves aligning the Qalb (heart), Aql (intellect), Nafs (behavioural inclinations), Jasad (physical body), and Ruh (spirit).

The Qalb's emotional source is central, and techniques like visualisation and breathing address emotions and foster spiritual connection through repentance (Tawbah).

The Aql engages in cognitive restructuring, and Zikr aligns thoughts with Islamic values. The Nafs is managed through Muhasabah, promoting self-discipline. The Jasad supports well-being through sunnah practices and a healthy lifestyle.

Lastly, the Ruh connects with Allah (SWT) with spiritual practices aiming for divine connection and balance. This integrated approach ensures holistic spiritual and mental well-being.

Chapter Four

Coping with Anxiety and Stress

Understanding anxiety and stress in light of Islamic teachings

In Islam, stress and anxiety are common human feelings that transcend all boundaries and cultural differences. Put simply, these feelings are a response to something that throws off our emotional or mental balance. In psychology, stress is defined as a sensation of pressure and strain. Anxiety is a strong emotion that arises naturally in reaction to stress.

They have the potential to become so oppressive that they keep you from moving forward in the aspects of your life that you most desire. Islam provides a unique perspective on managing and transcending these occasionally overwhelming emotions due to the relationship between spirituality and religion.

Anxiety is a common occurrence that is frequently triggered by stress. Islam offers some unique answers to this problem. Let's examine how!

Quranic remedies for alleviating worry and anxiety

Life is full of difficulties and trials. As stated by Allah (SWT) in the Quran:

> *"Do people think they will be left alone after saying 'We believe' without being put to the test?" (Quran 29:2)*

Regardless of one's strength or level of spiritual commitment, anxiety is a condition that affects everyone. While occasional anxiety is common, anxiety can be a debilitating mental condition for certain individuals. Taking care of one's mind, body, and soul is highly valued in Islamic heritage, and spiritual well-being is no less significant. Everybody faces challenges in life, and as Muslims, we should understand that these are tests from Allah (SWT).

> *In the Quran, Allah (SWT) says, "Do people think they will be left alone and they will not be tried?" (Quran 29:3)*

Many illnesses and afflictions have treatments in the Quran, which is the word of Allah (SWT) and contains them long before scientific investigation was done. Similarly, Allah (SWT) discusses human uneasiness and strategies for overcoming it in the Quran.

> *It is said in the Quran that "Indeed, mankind was created anxious" (Quran 70:9)*

There are many interpretations of this, but the primary one is that Allah (SWT) created humanity not for heaven but for this world. This indicates that the environment in which humans exist is abnormal. As a result, Allah's (SWT) creation experiences a wide range of emotions in this world. Humans experience both happy and negative emotions, such as worry and melancholy.

The Quran mentions dread, grief, and suffering as a part of life's challenges. On the other hand, total separation from those unpleasant feelings becomes a part of the ultimate recompense in the Hereafter.

> *"And certainly, We shall test you with something of fear, hunger, loss of wealth, lives and fruits, but give glad tidings to As-Sabirin (the patient ones, etc.)." (Quran 2:155)*

What exactly is anxiety?

Anxiety is commonly defined as an unpleasant emotion that affects everyone and is characterised by persistent tightness, nervousness, tenseness, or irritability.

Anxiety can have an impact on our thoughts and actions because it can keep us from accomplishing the things we need to and want to do. Even in cases where there is no reason to worry, anxiety makes us feel concerned for extended periods.

However, it's common to have anxiety or concern over certain aspects of life. Actually, it's frequently beneficial. For instance, thinking about how you'll pass an exam, pass your driving test, or ace the interview motivates you to study to prepare for the situation.

Occasionally, anxiety can trigger depression because persistent worry depletes your energy and breeds pessimistic ideas, which in turn triggers depression. Because depression reduces productivity, which eventually results in long-term concerns and anxiety, having depression may also create anxiety.

Symptoms of anxiety

Four types of signs might help you determine if you have anxiety: behavioural, emotional, mental, and physical.

- When it comes to ideas, you frequently ask yourself what would happen if anything terrible happened; you always consider the worst-case situation, your mind is constantly racing, and you worry continually.

- The possible physical symptoms you experience are tension, aches in the muscles, lightheadedness, chest pain, trembling, shivering, and palpitations are a few symptoms.

- When experiencing emotional symptoms, you frequently experience anxiety, panic, or tension, as well as feeling extremely agitated and short-tempered.

- And lastly, anxiety has behavioural signs. If you have a strong desire to avoid doing activities you enjoy, pace a lot, become easily frightened, speak too quickly, and lose your temper easily, you may have anxiety.

Practices to cope with anxiety

Islam views anxiety as a physical and mental response to fear. It's a mental health issue, a psychological issue. Instead of feeling anxious about the past, people tend to regret it and worry more about the present or the future, fearing that the past may recur. Islam's top recommendation for dealing with anxiety, tension, and worry—all of which are related—is to establish a relationship with Allah (SWT) and alter your fear-inspiring ideas.

Establishing a connection with Allah (SWT) eliminates feeling helpless about a situation. It encourages reliance on Allah (SWT) rather than solely on yourself for solutions. By mastering your thoughts, you can better regulate the mental and bodily responses associated with anxiety.

There are many doable strategies to manage your anxiety without allowing it to rule your life or become your greatest barrier. You could find that one of the methods on the following list of anxiety treatments is enough to get rid of your anxiety:

- **Turn to Allah (SWT)**

Making a call to Allah (SWT), the Most Powerful Almighty, is the most effective technique for overcoming anxiety. By means of regular prayer and Dua, Islam provides tranquillity and a connection with Allah (SWT).

Remembering Allah (SWT) can bring peace of mind, especially when faced with worries and fears. In these moments, we must never forget that Allah (SWT) is supremely strong, and nothing can defeat Him. Whatever we fear, there is nothing that Allah (SWT) cannot handle.

> *Allah (SWT) says in the Quran: "But whoever turns away from My Reminder will certainly have a miserable life, then we will raise them up blind on the Day of Judgment." (Quran 20:124)*

Allah (SWT) tells His followers that even with this dire warning, there is always room for repentance.

- **Adjust your goals**

Anxiety is frequently brought on by our expectations of what will happen or how things should be. When we realise that reality doesn't live up to our expectations, we start to fear failing and not getting our way. Our mind is aware of our expectations and is searching for indications that they will be fulfilled. When our expectations are not satisfied, our mind releases the stress hormone cortisol, making us anxious and afraid.

Changing your expectations, which genuinely cause you anxiety or a sense of fear in your life, is the simplest approach to control your stress levels. It can be managed or eliminated by just altering your expectations in your mind.

Most of the time, we foresee or predict significant obstacles in the road. Things will start to appear less stressful if you adjust your expectations and perspective.

- **Modifications to lifestyle to control anxiety**

Islam promotes a balanced lifestyle in addition to spiritual disciplines to preserve both physical and mental well-being. This includes having a balanced diet, regular exercise, getting enough sleep, and maintaining close social relationships—all of which can lessen anxiety symptoms.

- **Never compare yourself with others**

Our anxiety often stems from the fear of comparing ourselves to others. We constantly tell ourselves that we must compete with others because we see them as doing better, as being more successful. Instead, focus on your personal growth.

Aim to improve by just 1% each day. Avoid comparing yourself to individuals who are in a different stage of life than you. You were made to be exceptional, different, and fantastic at being who you are—not a copy of someone else.

- **Recite the Quran**

The lessons, precepts, and narratives found throughout the Quran impart eternal wisdom. Reading the Quran and thinking about its verses might facilitate putting one's troubles in perspective. The accounts of the Prophets and their tenacity in the face of innumerable hardships can encourage us to face our own challenges patiently.

Parallel to this, metaphors of Paradise and the prize for perseverance might help us get through difficult times.

Both the reciter and the listener gain much from reciting the Quran. Both offer limitless benefits, relief from anxiety-inducing circumstances, and healing.

> *In the Quran, Allah (SWT) declares: "O humanity! Indeed, there has come to you a warning from your Lord, a cure for what is in the hearts, a guide, and a mercy for the believers." (Quran 10:57)*

- **Make a dua for yourself**

As previously mentioned, connecting with Allah (SWT), the Almighty, is your most empowering action. The next most powerful action is constantly turning to Allah (SWT) and asking for assistance.

Most people spend their time begging Allah (SWT) to help them. But they're not taking any action. Thus, when action and dua are combined, an unstoppable force is created that will aid in our transformation.

Those who are struggling with anxiety can find comfort in the Quran-inspired cures listed. It cannot be overstated, though, that you should seek professional assistance if you or someone you love is experiencing persistent anxiety symptoms or warning indications of a severe anxiety condition.

In addition to providing faith-based remedies for our illnesses, our religion also provides workable answers that compassionately and empathetically address our humanity.

Practical coping strategies from the Sunnah

The Prophet Muhammad's (PBUH) customs and teachings, known as the Sunnah, provide insightful advice on managing stress and anxiety in particular and advancing general well-being. By applying these strategies, we can achieve calm and peace daily. Let's have a look at them!

Breathing exercises

Breathing exercises and relaxation techniques might also benefit stress management strategies. These techniques may ease your mind, relax your body, and slow your breathing. By incorporating these skills into your regular practice, you may manage stressful situations with composure and awareness.

Method of Deep Breathing (Tafakkur Nafas):

- Sit comfortably in a quiet place.
- Close your eyes and focus on your breath.
- Inhale deeply through your nose for a count of four.
- Hold your breath for a count of four.
- Exhale slowly through your mouth for a count of six.
- Repeat this cycle for 5-10 minutes.

Deep breathing helps oxygenate the brain, reduce stress, and promote a sense of calm.

Dhikr (Remembrance of Allah)

As Muslims, we are aware that worshipping Allah (SWT) alone is the ultimate goal of life. Thus, neglecting this fundamental need is one of the reasons for sadness and anxiety. If we're feeling anxious and can't figure out why, we ought to consider the possibility that we have been neglecting Allah's (SWT) memory.

> *The Holy Prophet (PBUH) declared: "No people stand up from a gathering in which they did not remember Allah (SWT) but that it is as if they have raised from the carcass of a donkey, and it will cause them grief." (Sunah Abu Dawud)*

It's easy to make it a habit to mention Allah (SWT) simply by incorporating phrases like SubhanAllah (Glory be to Allah SWT), Alhamdulillah (All praise is due to Allah SWT) and InshaAllah (If Allah SWT wills) into our everyday speech or after every prayer.

Learning the ninety-nine names of Allah (SWT) and calling out to Allah (SWT) by those names is another way to practise Dhikr. Constantly calling upon Allah (SWT) is an instant remedy for anxiety, as He mentions in the Quran:

> *"Surely in the remembrance of Allah (SWT) do hearts find comfort" (Quran 13:28)*

Mindfulness techniques

According to psychology, mindfulness is "a tool we can use to look into conceptual frameworks," which essentially means that we can confront our unhelpful thought patterns and ideas by examining them with the ability to stay present. We can try to identify the attitudes and actions that actually promote our well-being and apply them to our day-to-day activities.

The Islamic tradition is strongly ingrained in the Muraqabah ritual. "Muraqabah" derives from the verb "Raqaba", which means to watch, observe, and consider carefully. It is the practice of seeing oneself knowing that Allah (SWT) is fully aware of one's inner and outside realities.

Mindfulness, being present in the moment, is a practice encouraged in the Sunnah. The Prophet Muhammad (PBUH) advised focusing on the present and trusting Allah's (SWT) plan.

A youthful companion named Ibn Abbas (RA) received a timeless instruction from the Prophet (PBUH).

> *Ibn Abbas narrated: The Holy Prophet (PBUH) remarked to me as I was riding behind him one day: "Young man, I will teach you some words. Be mindful of Allah (SWT), and He will protect you. Be mindful of Allah (SWT), and you will find Him before you. If you ask, ask from Allah (SWT). If you seek help, seek help from Allah (SWT). Know that if the nations gathered together to benefit you, they could not benefit you unless Allah (SWT) has decreed it for you. And if the nations gathered together to harm you, they could not harm you unless Allah (SWT) has decreed it for you. The pens have been lifted, and the pages have dried." (Tirmidhi)*

Muraqabah has a deeper meaning in Islam than simply being aware of the present moment. It is a thorough understanding and method of remaining in contact with Allah (SWT). It comforts us that Allah is aware of our inner and outside lives, which benefits our mental and spiritual health. For Allah's (SWT) sake, it aids in our emotional self-control. It assists us in making wise choices for our Akhirah and Dunya. Muraqabah is a strategy that promotes appreciation for the present moment, enhances focus, and lowers stress.

Method of Mindful Observation:

- Find a quiet place and sit comfortably.
- Focus on a single object, such as a leaf or a flower.
- Observe its details: colour, shape, texture.
- Take slow, deep breaths as you observe.
- Reflect on Allah's (SWT) creation and feel a sense of wonder and connection.

Hence, by integrating these coping strategies from the life of the Holy Prophet (PBUH) into our daily routines, we can effectively manage stress, enhance our mental clarity, and develop a profound sense of inner peace and contentment.

Chapter Five

Overcoming Depression and Sadness

Addressing depression through Islamic perspectives

Depression is a mental illness marked by extreme negative feelings that affect a person's day-to-day functioning, such as melancholy, pessimism, or hopelessness. Sadness or sorrow is commonplace in life. Grief and depression are similar in that they both include deep sadness and seclusion, but they are not the same. Just as depression is diverse, there are many therapeutic choices available for it. Research has indicated that religious coping skills are one helpful type of treatment.

According to Islam, increasing spirituality can provide one with an inner power that makes it easier to have a peaceful, sensible perspective. The stereotype that depression represents a flaw in one's faith is unfounded when one considers that the Prophets and Companions also had periods of deep emotion and sadness, which is similar to what contemporary psychiatry equates with depression.

In light of this, Muslims can greatly benefit from the Quran's guidance in overcoming depression. Reciting and meditating on the Quran can help mitigate the full power of melancholy or sorrow brought on by life's challenges, struggles, and internal conflict, even though serious depression necessitates expert therapy.

The Quran frequently tells us that if we stay firm, there is no sorrow or dread and that the Hereafter is devoid of all those awful and oppressive emotions and circumstances. The Quran recognises the existence of these feelings and, thus, the existence of depression.

> *In the Quran, Allah (SWT) says: "So do not weaken and do not grieve, and you will be superior if you are [true] believers." (Quran 3:139)*

One gains an understanding of the value of faith and tenacity from this. This verse explains that although obstacles happen and giving in to feelings of helplessness is a normal reaction; one can still get back up after failing or facing the direst circumstances.

Islam offers its followers morals and behavioural guidelines that lend their lives direction and meaning. We must find a method to integrate Islamic ethics and values into psychotherapy, as a strong faith offers people hope, coping mechanisms, and ways to handle trying circumstances. This method helps people cope with stress and depression, strengthens their sense of belonging, and gives them access to a broader network of support when they're feeling hopeless and alone. A strong sense of spirituality also instils confidence, self-respect, and divine assistance.

Importance of seeking help and support in overcoming sadness

Islam plays a vital part in Muslims' lives by providing support in overcoming adversity and serving as a shield against and treatment for depression. It is important to get professional care for mental health disorders like depression, just like for any other sickness, as Muslims are not immune to them.

Islam constantly exhorts people to hold out hope since Allah's (SWT) mercy is always near, even in the darkest of situations or after committing the greatest sins. People should never lose hope, even in the face of the greatest sin or the most trying circumstance, for Allah's (SWT) mercy never ends.

> *"And never give up hope of Allah's (SWT) soothing Mercy: truly no one despairs of Allah's (SWT) soothing Mercy, except those who have no faith." (Quran 12:87)*

Because of this, we should be able to remember Allah (SWT) at difficult times and find hope in His compassion and kindness to help us get through the suffering. Islam's caring character and outlook make this possible.

Islam forbids suicide and views it as a grave sin, yet the situation is not clear-cut; we can recognise that a person suffering from a mental illness may have impaired judgement and may not be fully capable of making the right judgements. He or she might not be held responsible for their actions. The only one who can assess a person's behaviour is Allah (SWT). This kind of thinking can assist us in lessening the sense of guilt that typically accompanies mental health issues.

Grieving and sadness are normal aspects of being a human. They develop as a normal response to life's setbacks. Muslims hold that Allah (SWT) has predetermined all enjoyment, sorrow, death, and life. Allah (SWT) is the source of strength, and Allah (SWT) uses loss as a test to see what purpose we can make out of the pain and losses we endure. Our faith in Allah's (SWT) mercy is the goal. This kind of belief is very consoling and beneficial during the healing process.

Quranic Wisdom for Overcoming Depression

The Quran is one of the best places, a shelter for the pious, and one of the best ways to cope with stress after mishaps and calamities. If you're depressed, reading the following passages of the Quran will help you feel better. Reciting them and thinking about their meanings might help one feel better emotionally, understand or reinterpret their circumstances more clearly, and lessen depression.

- **Surah Al-Kahf**

This is the Quran's 18th chapter, renowned for its numerous benefits. Parables in this chapter address faith, knowledge, and power. These kinds of trials could be a factor in some people's depression. The stories in this collection impart life lessons about overcoming trials and adversities. These parables impart several moral lessons, including humility, thankfulness, patience, and persistence.

When faced with challenges, one should turn to Allah (SWT) for direction, for he can bestow the power and resources necessary to overcome the circumstances. The Quranic chapter underscores the boundless extent of the Creator's wisdom and power. It is stressed how important it is to remember Allah (SWT). Al-Kahf highlights the fact that Allah's (SWT) protection, compassion, and guidance are always present, which is one of its main points.

> *It is said that: "If the sea were ink for [writing] the words of my Lord, the sea would be exhausted before the words of my Lord were exhausted, even if we brought the like of it as a supplement." (Quran 18:109)*

Reciting and reflecting on Surah Al-Kahf might improve your mental health. Remember, when things get tough, try to figure out what you're being tested on and address it step by step.

- **Surah Ad-Duha**

The Quran's 93rd chapter was revealed to comfort Prophet Muhammad (PBUH) during a period when he felt anxious and depressed because of a delay in its revelation. The chapter's opening lyrics begin with swearing an oath by the light of day and the serenity of night in an expression of resounding reassurance, soothed the Prophet's distress.

One may encounter circumstances in this life that appear unfair or hopeless. When one feels totally alone, grief can take over one's life. This chapter offers insight into the reality that Allah (SWT) is dependable.

> *"Your Lord has not taken leave of you, [O Muhammad], nor has He detested [you]." (Quran 93:3)*

Surah ad-Duha was written to comfort Prophet Muhammad (PBUH) and give him hope that Allah (SWT) was with him; similarly, this chapter of the Quran can provide comfort to individuals experiencing comparable depressive, hopeless, or hopeless states.

Sadness and hardships are temporary in our world. This verse suggests that, in the greater scheme of things, the troubles we face in this life are transient. It causes one to change their perspective from one of present despair or anxiety to one of optimism for an optimistic future.

- **Surah Al-Inshirah**

The Quran's 94th chapter has themes of consolation and optimism. It was made public concurrently with Surah Duha. Surah Inshirah exhorts perseverance in the face of adversity and stress. At that time, Prophet Muhammad (PBUH) was in despair. Before becoming a prophet, he had not experienced his own people's severe and painful circumstances. The verses emphasise the need to take one's complaints to Allah (SWT) and promise that there will be relief after hardships. The Prophet (PBUH) is told in this passage that reliance on

Allah (SWT) and loyalty to Him increases one's capacity to withstand adversity.

> *"For indeed, with hardship [will be] ease. Indeed, with hardship [will be] ease." (Quran 94:5–6)*

The verse's repetition suggests that this is a given. One is given hope to overcome challenges like despair and grief, which is possible, just as the Prophet (PBUH) was guided and freed from his fears and hardships. This chapter of the Quran can ease emotional distress and bring peace of mind.

- **Surah An-Nas**

The Quran's 114th and last chapter is this one. It includes the idea of outside, invisible forces that have the power to corrupt people's hearts and minds. This chapter makes it possible to escape doubts, suspicions, and negative ideas.

Whispers from Satan can intensify self-doubt and negative thoughts, which are common components of depression and can become a cause of hopelessness, desperation, and debilitation. Reciting an-Nas frequently can prevent these tendencies from being ingrained, removing the chance that outside or invisible forces influence any persistent melancholy or hopelessness.

> *"Say, 'I seek refuge in the Lord of mankind...'" (Quran 114:1)*

And what is actually recited is a prayer asking the Creator for protection. Surah An-Nas also teaches a valuable coping strategy: the significance of both action and faith. It advises reciting to take affairs into one's own hands.

These few chapters and verses from the Quran can be a source of comfort, hope, and resilience for those experiencing depression. They remind us of the temporary nature of worldly troubles and the eternal support and guidance of Allah (SWT). The Quran offers profound guidance and solace, especially during times of depression.

Incorporating joy and positivity into daily life

In today's fast-paced and often stressful world, finding joy and positivity can be a vital component to maintaining mental and emotional health. Incorporating joy into our daily lives cannot be overstated; it not only enhances our overall well-being but also positively impacts our relationships, work performance, and even physical health. When we actively seek out and create moments of happiness, we build resilience against stress and adversity, cultivate a more optimistic outlook, and foster a more fulfilling life. Let's examine how it can be done using guidance from Islam.

Sunnah habits for fostering happiness and contentment

Each of us strives to attain the desired state of contentment, tranquillity, serenity, peace of mind, and absence of worries and anxieties. There are several ways to find happiness—religious, natural, and practical—but the only way to find ultimate happiness is to combine them all.

The most widely used definition of happiness is the ongoing state of joy, contentment, satisfaction, giving, and delight that results from being satisfied with oneself, one's life, and one's conviction that one will have a pleasant future. To be happy, a lot of people try to take complicated routes.

But they are blind to the simpler route, which is Islam. Sincere worship, striving to carry out morally upright behaviours, doing good deeds or charitable giving, and smiling at someone's face are all paths to happiness. These things have the capacity to provide us with genuine happiness.

As most of us have come to realise, happiness is the feeling of contentment and peacefulness. Therefore, the key to attaining true happiness is to be contented and experience the peace of body, mind and soul. Contentment is a marker of happiness, richness, self-sufficiency, and tranquillity. Contentment is one of the acts of worship of the heart.

According to Islamic belief, happiness is a lifetime process that aims to bring about eternal tranquillity of mind, tranquillity of heart, contentment in this world, and everlasting bliss in the Hereafter. It is not just a fleeting condition of joy and enjoyment.

> *The Prophet (PBUH) said: "He has tasted the sweetness of faith who is content with Allah (SWT) as his Lord, Islam as his religion, and Muhammad PBUH as his Prophet." (Sahih Muslim)*

Happiness in life is rooted in contentment, a quality many regrettably lack. Trusting our creator, who manages our affairs, is the path to genuine happiness. We must believe Allah (SWT) always has our best interests at heart. Contentment brings about wholehearted enjoyment, inner serenity, and calmness. Contentment is the key to drawing closer to Allah (SWT) in this life and the next.

By incorporating the Sunnah habits below into our daily lives, we can achieve a balanced and fulfilling sense of happiness and contentment.

- **Gratitude Exercise**

Gratitude is a great way to stay motivated and have an optimistic outlook. Every day, set aside some time to consider the benefits that Allah (SWT) has placed upon you. Write down everything you are thankful for in a gratitude journal. Be thankful in your prayers and cultivate the practice of thanking Allah (SWT) for all His blessings. Gratitude creates motivation and a happy heart.

> *The Holy Prophet (PBUH) has said: "Whoever is not grateful for small things will not be grateful for large things." (Ahmad)*

This underscores the significance of gratitude in our daily interactions and relationship with our creator, fostering motivation and a content heart.

- **Adopt Balance and Self-Care**

Maintaining motivation requires good care of your psychological, emotional, and physical well-being. Make self-care activities a priority, including getting enough sleep, exercising, eating well, and pursuing enjoyable hobbies. Maintaining a healthy balance between your commitments and duties ensures you have time for introspection, rest, and renewal.

> *The Prophet Muhammad (PBUH) said: "Your body has a right over you, your eyes have a right over you, and your wife has a right over you." (Sahih Bukhari)*

This Hadith highlights the necessity of fulfilling various rights, including caring for oneself.

- **Embrace the Positive Influences**

Our social circle has a big impact on our attitude and drive. Be in the company of positive, like-minded people who encourage and inspire you. Look for neighbourhoods, Islamic centres, or online communities that support spirituality, personal development, and moral principles.

Participate in conversations, exchange personal stories, and find inspiration in the encouragement and support of other Muslims.

- **Adhere to the Teachings of the Prophet (PBUH)**

Examine and model the life of the Prophet Muhammad (PBUH). He was the picture of patience, thankfulness, and satisfaction in the face of great adversity.

Our faith provides us Muslims with a special source of inspiration. We can develop a lively and long-lasting motivation by applying these techniques to our everyday lives. Establish a prayerful connection with Allah (SWT), pursue knowledge, make significant goals, cultivate thankfulness, be in the company of positive people, and value self-care. Recall that maintaining motivation is a lifelong journey and that we can find inspiration and meaning in all facets of our lives by following the teachings of Islam.

Encouraging social connections and community involvement

Engaging in communal activities enhances unity by providing a feeling of purpose and belonging. Islam strongly emphasises community living and social contact, supporting the development of brotherhood and sisterhood among believers. Islam acknowledges that each person has a distinct personality and recognises the value of respecting each person's choice as it promotes social gatherings.

> The Quran teaches, "Indeed, the believers are brothers and sisters, so make peace between your brothers and sisters." (Quran 49:10)

The Holy Prophet (PBUH) was renowned for showing mercy and kindness to everyone, regardless of individual differences.

> *He said, "Allah (SWT) is kind, and He loves kindness and confers upon kindness which he does not confer upon severity." (Sahih Muslim)*

Moreover, Islam urges followers to locate other believers who share their beliefs and create a community centred on shared interests.

> *The Prophet Muhammad (PBUH) said, "A person is rewarded for the good deeds done by his companions" (Sahih Bukhari)*

Ultimately, Islam urges believers to appreciate one another's decisions and acknowledges the distinctive personality features of every person. Although interacting with others is encouraged, it is crucial to do so in a way that complements each person's unique personality. Islamic teachings emphasise that connecting with like-minded people and striking a balance between community and solitude can enhance one's sense of belonging and general well-being.

Chapter Six

Seeking Spiritual Healing

Role of spirituality in mental health recovery

Seeking care choices that support our mental health and spiritual well-being may be most advantageous when we're dealing with emotional upheaval and mental health difficulties. Religiosity is claimed to be the best predictor of favourable mental health outcomes, such as life satisfaction, meaning in life, and general well-being.

Islamically integrated mental health care can address not only the psychological upheaval we are experiencing but also the spiritual core or beating heart.

What is spirituality?

Spirituality can be conceptualised in a variety of ways. One way to look at it is in terms of the purpose and significance you seek out in life. It ought to help you realise how valuable and worthwhile you are. Some examples of spiritual practices are as follows:

- Being a part of a religious group

- Prayer and meditation
- Emphasising spiritual principles like compassion, kindness, honesty, and optimism.
- Following a set of guidelines that you establish for yourself. Consider the way you handle others.

Religion and spirituality are intertwined. However, spirituality can encompass a wider range of activities. To various people, it may mean different things. You may also adhere to a shared spiritual conviction.

Spirituality does not require religiosity. With the aid of religion and spirituality, you can grow inner strength, inner tranquillity, inner hope, and optimism.

How can spirituality and religion be beneficial when a person has a mental illness?

Religion and spirituality can be powerful tools for navigating difficult situations and enhancing mental well-being.

- Being part of a religious or spiritual community can provide meaningful friendships and a strong support network.
- Feeling a part of something greater than yourself could benefit you and help you make sense of what you have experienced.
- You might experience a greater sense of harmony with others and yourself.
- Your spirituality or religion can instil courage or hope, which can be especially significant when you're sick.

In Islam, mental and spiritual health is of utmost importance. It's common to understand that we are unable to execute our obligations to Allah (SWT) if we are ill. Hence, it is crucial to practise holistic self-care, which includes comprehending human nature from an Islamic standpoint.

Because the Quran and Hadith of the Prophet Muhammad (PBUH) instruct and guide Muslims to adhere to specific principles when they are in distress or suffer calamities and life challenges, Islam prioritises the practice of religious ritual practices in healing stress and mental diseases. Let's have a look at this!

Utilising prayer (salah) and supplication (dua) for emotional healing

Role of Prayer (Salah)

Prayer is a cornerstone of religious devotion for Muslims, who must offer five daily prayers to establish a spiritual connection with Allah (SWT) Almighty.

> *Allah (SWT) says in the Quran, "Maintain with care the [obligatory] prayers and [in particular] the middle prayer and stand before Allah (SWT), devoutly obedient." (Quran 2:238)*

Let's examine how everyday Islamic prayers improve people's general well-being. The Islamic prayer, Salah, is a potent instrument that promotes awareness and the harmonious blending of the material and spiritual realms. Through its many elements, including motions, recitations, and intentions, people develop a more conscious understanding of their bodies and their relationship to the divine.

This link between the mind and body promotes calmness, reduces stress, and enhances general well-being. Muslims can develop a sense of peace and tranquillity by reading the passages and performing the postures with awareness.

Thus, Salah becomes a practice that transforms and enhances people's lives by simultaneously nourishing their spiritual and physical selves.

Psychological Benefits of Salah

- **Stress Reduction**

Muslims use their daily prayers to gain comfort and inner serenity. The recitation of Holy verses and rhythmic movements create a quiet environment that eases anxiety and encourages mental relaxation.

Prayer has been demonstrated in numerous studies to offer physiological effects, including a reduction in stress hormones and blood pressure. It provides Muslims with a place to go to receive comfort, reaffirm their faith, and gather the courage to confront life's hardships with a calm heart.

> *The Prophet Muhammad (PBUH) said, "O Bilal, call (the people) to prayer, let us find comfort in it." (Sunah Abu Dawood)*

- **Focus and Mental Clarity**

Prayer calms the mind and improves concentration; the purposeful movements and utterances that make up prayer offer a structure that enables people to disengage from external disturbances and enter a calm, spiritual state.

By developing a disciplined prayer routine, believers can get the comprehensive benefits of increased mental engagement, inner peace, and a closer bond with their faith. Prayer requires mental presence and concentration in order to pray in an Islamic manner.

> *The Prophet Muhammad (PBUH) said, "When any one of you stands for prayer, he is speaking in private to his Lord, so he should pay attention to how he speaks to Him." (Sahih Bukhari)*

- **Control of Emotions**

Prayer is an organised channel for expressing feelings and asking a higher power for comfort. Muslims find consolation in prayer during hard times, as it helps them process their negative feelings, find peace, and gain a new perspective.

Prayer has been linked to improved mental resilience, elevated emotional intelligence and regulation. It allows believers to express and deal with their feelings, promoting inner calm and harmony.

People who connect with a higher power gain the strength to get through difficult situations and have a deeper knowledge of their emotions. Therefore, prayer is essential for promoting spiritual development and emotional well-being.

> *"Indeed, prayer prohibits immorality and wrongdoing, and the remembrance of Allah (SWT) is greater." (Quran 29:45)*

- **Tool for managing time**

Time blocking is one way that participating in Islamic prayer can help people learn effective time management. By setting aside designated times for each prayer during the day, Muslims can create a regimented schedule that prioritises their spiritual responsibilities.

Time blocking encourages one to set aside certain times for prayer while effectively managing other obligations. By encouraging discipline and increasing awareness of daily routines, this practice eventually supports a healthy, productive existence.

As a result, Salah promotes efficient time management and acts as a channel for spiritual connection.

Hence, Salah is not merely an Islamic ritual but a profound practice that intertwines life's physical, mental, and spiritual aspects. Through prayer, Muslims can achieve a harmonious balance between their worldly duties and spiritual obligations, leading to a more fulfilled and peaceful existence.

Ultimately, Salah is a transformative practice that nurtures the body and soul, guiding believers towards a life of purpose, clarity, and inner peace.

Role of Supplication (Dua)

Dua is a way of asking Allah (SWT) for aid or support. It is considered a significant act of worship for Muslims. The efficacy of dua can offer comfort in difficult circumstances. Include dua in your self-care practice and seek wisdom, courage, and serenity from Allah.

Muslims are endowed with strong and potent duas that can reduce tension and anxiety while bringing us closer to Allah (SWT). You can use the following few succinct yet powerful duas every day to help you stay composed and find solace during tough times:

- **To safeguard yourself from anxiety and depression**

    Holy Prophet (PBUH) said, "O Allah (SWT), I take refuge in You from anxiety and sorrow, weakness and laziness, miserliness and cowardice, the burden of debts and from being overpowered by men." (Sahih Bukhari)

- **Dua to alleviate worries**

    "O Living and Eternal Maintainer! By Your mercy, I seek help!" (Tirmidhi)

- **Dua to remove debt-related stress**

"O Allah (SWT), suffice me with what you have allowed instead of what You have forbidden, and make me independent of all others besides You." *(Tirmidhi)*

- **Dua for patience**

"There is no deity, but you. Glory be to You! Verily, I have been among the wrongdoers." *(Quran 21:87)*

Incorporating these powerful duas into your daily routine will help you navigate life's challenges and strengthen your connection with Allah (SWT).

Strengthening faith as a source of inner peace

Islam ranks faith as a highly important factor. To become a Muslim, a person needs to testify this phrase: "I bear witness that there is no god but Allah (SWT), and I bear witness that Muhammad is the Messenger of Allah (SWT)." This is the Shahada, the Islamic declaration of faith. Even if a Muslim has never seen Allah (SWT) or Muhammad (PBUH), they must hold this belief to become a true Muslim.

Muslims also acknowledge every prophet sent by Allah (SWT) to teach humanity. The Holy Prophet Muhammad (PBUH) is considered the last messenger of Allah (SWT), and the Quran is the last revealed book from Allah (SWT). Revered as the holy book of Islam, the Quran has been preserved in its original form for over 1,400 years.

Muslims who have faith in Allah (SWT) can be patient during difficult times and express gratitude for their blessings because they know that nothing happens without Allah's (SWT) permission. Faith in Allah

(SWT) can be a powerful source of inner peace for Muslims. Believing in a higher power and trusting in divine wisdom and guidance provides comfort and stability.

Faith can be a potent ally in the battle against depression, as faith provides emotional and spiritual support. Engaging in regular religious rituals provides a comforting structure and routine. These practices also offer moments of reflection and connection with Allah (SWT), fostering a sense of peace and stability.

Depression is a real, crippling illness that can affect anyone, regardless of ethnicity or faith. However, by strengthening their faith in Allah (SWT), Muslims can take proactive measures to prevent and manage it.

Importance of connecting with Allah (SWT) to nurture mental well-being

As Muslims, we should recognise the significance of maintaining a close relationship with Allah (SWT) as it is not only beneficial for our spiritual health but also positively affects day-to-day living. It provides the fortitude and resiliency needed to keep going in the face of difficulties.

Sincere commitment and dedication to our faith are necessary for developing a relationship with Allah (SWT). It entails admitting our own frailties and limits and pleading for Allah's (SWT) pardon and mercy. It also entails making a deliberate effort to better ourselves and the people around us and living our lives in line with Islamic principles.

> *In the Quran, Allah (SWT) says: "And whoever turns away from My remembrance - indeed, he will have a depressed (difficult) life, and We will gather him on the Day of Resurrection blind." (Quran 20:124)*

Regular prayer and Quran recitation remind us of our life's purpose and the ideals and standards we ought to pursue. Through these acts of worship, we can meet and talk to Allah (SWT) and ask for His blessings and help. Establishing a deep connection with Allah (SWT) requires intentional measures to develop our faith.

We can also fortify our relationship with Allah (SWT) by performing deeds of love and generosity. Not only does helping the less fortunate benefit them, but it also purifies our spirits, strengthens our faith, and increases our humility.

> *The Prophet Muhammad (PBUH) said, "The strong believer is better and more beloved to Allah (SWT) than the weak believer, while there is good in both. Strive for that which benefits you, seek help from Allah (SWT), and do not be impatient." (Sahih Muslim)*

Developing a relationship with Allah (SWT) is a personal path that necessitates us taking charge of maintaining our religion. By dedicating our lives to Allah (SWT) and His teachings, we may lead meaningful lives, inspire and mentor people around us, and realise our own desires.

We must remember that life's primary purpose is to become closer to Allah (SWT) because we are from Allah and must return to Him. We must also remember that the truth of getting close to him is not a straightforward and easy path. It calls for strong faith and steady efforts.

> *The Messenger (PBUH) said: "There lies within the body a piece of flesh. If it is sound, the whole body is sound, and if it is corrupted, the whole body is corrupted. Verily, this piece is the heart." (Sahih Muslim)*

First and foremost, we must get to know Allah before developing a heart connected to Him. The Quran is one of the many means through which Allah has provided us with a smooth way to get advice anytime we need it. Moreover, spending time reciting and contemplating His Names, which we learn from the Quran and Sunnah, is another approach to getting to know Allah Almighty.

From His names, we understand that Allah (SWT) is Al-Khaliq (the One who created us and everything we might possibly want), As-Sami' (the One who hears all of our prayers), and Al-Qadir (the One who can do anything, no matter how unattainable it may appear to our finite vision). Each of these names guides us on the path to drawing closer to Him.

By reflecting on and learning about Allah's us to build a positive foundation for our connection with Allah (SWT) and make it one we are happy to work on and dedicate ourselves to. So, investigate, educate yourself, and consider Allah's (SWT) Names.

Mend your heart to get closer to Allah (SWT). As humans, our hearts may eventually break or cause us to feel empty within. Instead of attempting to replace this emptiness with anything else, we must learn to fill it with a personal relationship with Allah (SWT).

Having faith that Allah (SWT) will accept your contrition. In the Quran, He speaks of His forgiveness far more frequently than His punishment. We all make mistakes from time to time, but it's important to recognise them and turn to Allah right away.

Since repentance is ongoing, getting back on track could require multiple attempts. Nevertheless, no matter how serious the transgression is, don't be ashamed to return to Him, and never give up on His boundless mercy.

Nothing is more important to us than prayer when purifying our hearts. One way to think of the five daily prayers is as an ongoing reminder of our faith. If we intentionally participate in our prayers, it revitalises us spiritually. Furthermore, Allah (SWT) says in the Quran that remembering Him brings the deepest serenity and calm to our hearts. Prayer and the Quran are the best sources for keeping our hearts spiritually alive.

All you need to do is never miss your prayer, offer all prayers on time, and set a specific time to recite and reflect on the Quran, even if it's just one verse daily. The most crucial thing is finding a time that suits you best and sticking to it regularly.

Your perception of the world around you is a function of your heart's condition. We must take care of our hearts as we do with our bodies and intellect to have a personal connection with Allah (SWT).

Chapter Seven

Building Resilience and Inner Strength

Developing psychological resilience through Islamic teachings

Gaining resilience and the capacity to adjust and bounce back from difficulties is an essential life skill for any Muslim. Islam offers a distinctive viewpoint on resilience, highlighting the significance of patience, persistence, and faith in Allah (SWT) in overcoming life's obstacles.

Maintaining mental resilience in a time of uncertainty, stress, and misfortune is more important than ever. Islam provides priceless ideas and customs that support this enduring power. The ability to rise to obstacles in life with dignity and tenacity is known as resilience.

As we've seen, Islamic teachings tell us that this world serves as a test for our spiritual resilience or patience and that we should work to develop it.

Allah (SWT) tells us, "...do you think that you shall enter heaven without being tried..." (Quran 2:214)

We should admit that every circumstance provides advantages for the believer; during easy times, the believer expresses gratitude to Allah (SWT), and during difficult times, the believer demonstrates endurance and patience.

As a result, the believer is always in a condition of thankfulness or patience, which leads to reflection, humility, and generosity. The good news is that a resilient mindset and attitude can be developed even if a person is not naturally resilient.

Creating an environment of resilience, strength, and patience requires you to remember certain things, regardless of whether you have experienced the loss of your loved ones, riches, safety, or sense of self-worth. The following are essential to establishing a mindset and setting that fosters spiritual resilience.

Remember that you're human and may occasionally experience low self-esteem. The only way you can truly strive towards improving yourself is if you accept that as a human, it's very natural. Thus, remember that Allah (SWT) is the Forgiving, even if you say or do something you regret. For as long as you live, there is still hope for you to make amends. The patience and consistency are still available to you.

And Allah (SWT) is aware of our many shortcomings and our inherent flaws; even the finest men and women in Islamic history experienced grief and intense emotions just like us. Yes, during their painful moments, they did and said things they later regretted.

The account of Hazrat Maryam (AS) giving birth to Hazrat Isa (AS) is among the best illustrations of this. Allah (SWT) declares:

> *"And the pains of childbirth drove her to the trunk of a palm tree. She said: Oh, I wish I had died before this and was in oblivion, forgotten." (Quran 19:23)*

Her pleas were not met with a stern command from Allah (SWT), "Do not wish for death!" or "Have more patience!" Instead, it was said to her as an act of immense and incredible mercy:

> *"...Do not grieve; your Lord has provided beneath you a stream. And shake toward you the trunk of the palm tree; it will drop upon you ripe, fresh dates. So eat and drink and be contented." (Quran 19:24-26)*

How kind Allah (SWT) is to have provided us with a real, human example of a woman who was in such agony that she begged to die.

Remember that this was not just any woman—this was Maryam (AS), the most admirable and morally upright believing woman in Islamic history. Allah (SWT) shows us how He answered, "Do not grieve," in a way that was reassuring, kind, and loving.

Thus, acknowledge that you're a human and that you will experience low points from time to time. The only way you can truly strive towards improving yourself is to adopt resilience.

We have a wealth of historical evidence of prophets and pious individuals who have experienced a wide range of emotions; nonetheless, what always won these individuals Allah's (SWT) affection was their ability to use their unique circumstances to worship Him in a more comprehensive and meaningful way.

> *The Quran states, "And seek help through patience and prayer, and indeed, it is difficult except for the humbly submissive [to Allah SWT]." (Quran 2:45)*

This verse highlights the value of prayer and patience when asking for assistance when things are tough. Muslims are urged to seek Allah's (SWT) assistance and direction in overcoming life's obstacles.

The Quran must be a central component of our lives to develop spiritual and emotional strength. There is no other transient pleasure like the happiness that arises from genuinely connecting with Allah's (SWT) teachings.

The Quran is a constant source of help and relief, but only those who have carried it with them as a travelling companion can truly appreciate it.

It might be challenging to see the bright side of things or the glass half full. But if you look closely enough, you'll see that Allah (SWT) has bestowed upon you so much, even throughout your worst and most trying times.

Even a challenge you detest may ultimately turn out to be advantageous. In the Quran, Allah (SWT) states as follows:

> *"But perhaps you hate a thing, and it is good for you; and perhaps you love a thing and it is bad for you. And Allah (SWT) Knows, while you know not." (Quran 2:216)*

It's crucial for your mental health to take the time to deliberately and fully recall all of the blessings Allah (SWT) has bestowed upon you. Every day, record it in a thankfulness notebook. Make it a habit to take time each day to consider your blessings, large and small.

> *Allah (SWT) says in the Quran: "And remember! your Lord caused to be declared (publicly): 'If ye are grateful, I will add more (favours) unto you'." (Quran 14:7)*

Allah (SWT) appreciates your thanks to Him and rewards you for it. Worshipping Him involves acknowledging His favours and blessings. In Allah's (SWT) eyes, one genuine, authentic "Alhamdulillah" is more valuable than a mountain of money. And you'll feel happier all around.

Moreover, the foundation of Islamic resilience is the idea of Sabr (patience). Muslims are expected to trust Allah's (SWT) plan and show patience and endurance in the face of hardship.

> *The Quran states, "Indeed, Allah (SWT) is with the patient." (Quran 2:153)*

This verse emphasises how crucial patience and tenacity are to success and conquering obstacles.

In Islam, the Prophet Muhammad (PBUH) is a prime example of fortitude. Throughout his life, he had many difficulties and setbacks, yet he never wavered in his commitment to his purpose and religion.

> *The Prophet Muhammad (PBUH) said, "Strange are the ways of a believer, for there is good in every affair of his, and this is not the case with anyone else except in the case of a believer: if he has an occasion to feel delight, he thanks (Allah SWT), thus there is a good for him in it, and if he gets into trouble and shows resignation (and endures it patiently), there is a good for him in it." (Sahih Muslim)*

This Hadith highlights the need for resilience in Islam and the ability of a believer to find the good in every circumstance, whether it be a happy or tough one. Islam also stresses the importance of cultivating an optimistic outlook to foster resilience. Muslims are urged to emphasise the good things in their lives and express gratitude to Allah (SWT) for their benefits.

Islam also highlights the value of community support in fostering resilience. Muslims are urged to assist one another in hard times and to ask for assistance from others when necessary. Muslims are always advised to put their faith in Allah (SWT) and work hard to better their circumstances.

> *The Quran states, "Indeed, Allah (SWT) will not change the condition of a people until they change what is in themselves." (Quran 13:11)*

This verse highlights the significance of acting to make things better while acknowledging Allah's (SWT) supreme sovereignty.

Developing resilience is an essential talent for everyone to have to succeed in life. Islam offers a distinctive viewpoint on resilience by highlighting the significance of having faith in Allah (SWT), being patient and persistent, cultivating an optimistic outlook, and having the support of one's community. Muslims can tackle life's obstacles with confidence and strength by adhering to Islamic principles, building resilience, and having faith in Allah's (SWT) purpose for their lives.

Lessons in patience (Sabr) and perseverance from the lives of the Prophets

There will be tests for every believer who follows Allah (SWT). Nobody can live a perfectly happy life devoid of challenges. Even though we have firsthand experience with how unexpected this world can be, the uncertainty of every moment still surprises us. It's in these moments that we discover the reality of life. However, the outcome depends on how we handle them. A difficult time does not indicate that Allah (SWT) is ignoring us; rather, it draws us closer to the Almighty.

> *The Prophet Muhammad (PBUH) said: "If Allah (SWT) wants to do good to somebody, He afflicts him with trials." (Sahih Bukhari)*

The life we lead here is a preparation for the life to come in the next world. To rejoice in the afterlife, believers must labour hard in the here and now. Allah (SWT) places obstacles in our way to make us examine our own faith and lead us closer to Himself. In these trying times, believers try to be patient to be blissful in heaven.

> *Indeed, Allah (SWT) says: "And whatever strikes you of disaster it is for what your hands have earned — but He pardons much." (Quran 42:30)*

In Islam, patience is highly valued in the eyes of Allah (SWT). The greatest fruit of acts is patience, which has endless rewards. Within Islam, patience or Sabr is a highly valued quality. It is among the most cherished and authentic types of worship. By keeping Sabr, we sincerely accept all that Allah (SWT) has penned for us and dedicate ourselves to His Will.

> *"And be patient and persevering, for Allah (SWT) is with those who patiently persevere." (Quran 8:46)*

Sabr literally translates to "bear," "enduring," "resisting pain, suffering, and difficulty," and "handling problems calmly." More broadly, it refers to one of the most crucial heart-related virtues that the Quran mentions.

> *Prophet Muhammad (PBUH) said: "Strange indeed are the affairs of the believers, for all their affairs are good for them... If good things happen to them, they're thankful, and that is good for them; and if bad things happen to them, they remain patient, and that too is good for them." (Sahih Muslim)*

Because of its significance, patience is considered half of one's religious life. (Gratitude makes up the other half.) It is a quality that helps us pursue admirable objectives and be unfazed by challenging circumstances.

There are numerous difficulties in life, and regrettably, there are still people who deal with far more difficulties than we do. The greatest challenges of all are those posed by poverty and war; realising this and acting to alleviate their plight purifies the soul. Islam does not forbid expressing one's feelings in response to a loss or disappointment, even if it promotes patience.

Being loved by Allah (SWT) is one of the greatest joys in this life and the next. To be patient is to be loved by The Most Loving.

> *"How many of the prophets fought (in Allah's SWT way), and with them (fought) large bands of [religious] men? But they never lost heart if they met with disaster in Allah's SWT way, nor did they weaken (in will) nor give in. And Allah (SWT) Loves those who are firm and steadfast." (Quran 3:146)*

We must have faith that Allah (SWT) is always there to support us when we confront challenges and go through difficult periods in life. As a result, we must exercise patience and ask for His assistance in prayer.

The entire Quran is incredibly beautiful. The significance of Sabr can be inferred from the numerous verses that directly or indirectly discuss the virtue of patience. The fact that Allah (SWT) uses the word "Sabr" in all of its guises multiple times throughout the Quran indicates how important it is. The following verses from the Quran discuss patience:

> *"O believers! Seek comfort in patience and prayer. Allah (SWT) is truly with those who are patient." (Quran 2:153)*

> *"And seek help through patience and prayer; and indeed, it is difficult except for the humbly submissive [to Allah SWT]. (Quran 2:45)*

> *"And be patient, [O Muḥammad], and your patience is not but through Allah (SWT). And do not grieve over them and do not be in distress over what they conspire". (Quran 16:127)*

The Holy Quran emphasises the importance of comprehending patience to achieve virtue. While exercising and demonstrating patience is a difficult skill, when done sincerely, it can be the most fruitful of all.

> *The Prophet Muhammad (PBUH) said: "How wonderful is the affair of the believer, for his affairs are all good, and this applies to no one but the believer. If something good happens to him, he is thankful for it, and that is good for him. If something bad happens to him, he bears it with patience, and that is good for him." (Sahih Muslim)*

No matter how minor it may seem, Allah (SWT) removes our sins and rewards us for every uncomfortable moment we go through as long as we remain patient. Furthermore, facing challenges now on Earth is far preferable to suffering punishment hereafter.

> *The Prophet (PBUH) said: "If Allah (SWT) intends good for His servant, He hastens the punishment for him in this world." (Tirmidhi)*

> *Furthermore, the Prophet (PBUH) said: "The believing men and women continue to experience trials in their lives, with their children and wealth until they meet Allah (SWT) without any sin." (Tirmidhi)*

The Patience Stories in the Quran

Islam emphasises patience, and we are taught to be patient with whatever comes our way. Prophet Ayub (AS) was put to the test by Allah (SWT) in a way that ultimately cost him his health. His tongue and heart were the only parts of his body that historians claimed were immune to sickness, but he constantly recalled Allah (SWT) and kept patience.

Prophet Nuh (AS) only attracted 11–80 followers despite spending nearly 950 years spreading his heavenly word. Throughout his battle for propagation, he frequently encountered mistreatment, mockery, and occasionally total stupidity. However, he persisted in waiting amiably for the results of his labours. Then, when the great flood submerged the rest of the earth, he and his followers set sail for Mount Judi.

> *"And certainly We sent Noah to his people, so he remained among them a thousand years save fifty years. And the deluge overtook them while they were unjust. So we delivered him and the Companions of the Ark. And We made it a sign for all peoples." (Quran 29:14–15)*

This demonstrates how much Allah (SWT) values endurance. The believer always prioritises everything in life because of his true faith in Allah (SWT), believing that whatever happens is for the greater good. When relief arrives, he gives gratitude to Allah (SWT). He also turns to Allah (SWT) in times of adversity.

Sometimes, when our patience does not yield the desired outcome, we could feel hopeless. Indeed, Allah (SWT) teaches us that patient people belong to the excellent deeds whose benefits are assured. Hence, there are many benefits to practising Sabr and having patience! Therefore, we should view it as a means of pleading with Allah (SWT) for mercy.

> *The Prophet Muhammad (PBUH) said that: "True patience is at the first stroke of calamity." (Sahih Bukhari)*

Islam instructs and leads us in all areas of life since it is a comprehensive rule of conduct. Thus, it teaches us to be patient in the face of adversity because we have a firm trust in the Almighty Allah (SWT), who we know will never abandon us.

Cultivating a positive mindset and self-empowerment

Keeping a positive outlook in a society where difficulties and uncertainty frequently cast a shadow cannot be overlooked. Not only can positivity influence our personal lives, but it also significantly affects our professional lives. It strengthens resilience, improves well-being, and cultivates deep relationships.

When we pay attention to the positive aspects instead of concentrating on the bad, we are more likely to see their beneficial aspects. This can support our ability to maintain motivation and move forward in adversity. It also helps us hold onto hope and optimism, which can be tremendously empowering.

Leaning into the timeless wisdom that inspires believers to embrace optimism, let's unveil the teachings of Islam, which serve as a beacon of hope for millions of people. These lessons light the way, just as they are symbols of hope and light.

Positive thinking can significantly affect our general well-being and how we manage life. A positive mindset involves approaching obstacles with optimism and concentrating on the positive aspects of our lives. Due to our appreciation of the good things that have happened to us, having an optimistic viewpoint makes us feel better and more fulfilled. Additionally, it makes it possible for us to deal with problems skillfully since we're more likely to overcome obstacles and grow from failures rather than give up.

For better or worse, our thoughts can strongly influence our emotional states and sentiments, influencing our actions. Islam instructs us to focus our acts of contemplation, or deep thinking, on the names and qualities of Allah (SWT), his signs, his wonders and benefits, optimism, and hope for the Hereafter. A positive mind helps us overcome the anger, depression, and anxiety that come from thinking about the outside world. It also makes our prayers and worship more powerful.

Islam asserts that the mind's power is derived from its thoughts, as the Quran teaches. Your thoughts define who you are. An optimistic perspective on life depends on having positive views about the world because your thoughts shape your perspective.

If you think negatively, you're more inclined to have a pessimistic outlook on life, directly impacting your life's quality. According to the Quran, Allah (SWT) states that ideas—especially thinking about Allah (SWT)—are the source of contentment and emotions of calm.

How to begin it?

Take a start when you wake up in the morning. The first thing we should do when we wake up, according to the teachings of the Holy Prophet (PBUH), is to think positively about Allah (SWT). That is to express gratitude to Allah (SWT) for giving you life and each new day to live a life filled with greatness.

Gratitude will make you happy. The fact that you have another opportunity in life is the greatest blessing because so many people go to sleep and never wake up again. Take advantage of the fresh opportunities that arise every day.

Avoid becoming lost in the daily grind of life. Recall Allah (SWT), and then once more when you have finished your Fajr salah. Every morning, take a triple dosage of positivity. If you think gratitude and happy thoughts daily, consider the benefits they could have for you. That would be sufficient to give you a wonderful start to each day of your life.

Do the morning Adhkar and follow the Prophet's (PBUH) sunnah; this will naturally set up your frame of mind and give you an optimistic, completely positive thought process and outlook throughout the day.

Satan (the devil) will occasionally implant malicious ideas in our heads. Unless we decide to take action on them, they should not influence us. A tragic conclusion awaits us if we follow a negative or bad thought. Therefore, to counteract the negative thoughts that catch us off guard, we must quickly switch them out with affirmations from within.

After we become aware of the consequences of both good and negative thoughts, we must learn to divert our minds from negative ideas and ignore them before they send us into a downward spiral.

Remind yourself of the advantages of positivism

- Individuals become optimistic when they start thinking positively about their lives and themselves. This optimism will impact how we view other people as well. Finding the good in every circumstance makes us more tolerant and forgiving and allows us to glance past others.

- Greater chance of discovering positive options in relationships, employment, and lifestyle

- Greater patience and a decreased propensity to respond negatively to life's experiences

- Higher levels of happiness and well-being

- Enhanced vitality and drive to perform acts of kindness and benefit.

Islam instructs us to disregard negative ideas and focus our attention on the positive. We merely pursue concepts that should be nice or, at the very least, neutral, just like external words. To counteract the negative impact of thought, we should follow it with many affirmations directed inside. Thinking positively should result in an upbeat attitude and high hopes for Allah (SWT) and his kindness. These positive aspirations are the inner key that unlocks the full potential of our prayers and worship.

Never doubt that Allah has a purpose for your life; even if anything goes wrong, it will most likely turn out well. Despite maybe not feeling it initially, HE is taking care of you. Be grateful and have trust. Miracles flourish when faith and hope develop!

Importance of self-empowerment

Being in charge of your own future is a deliberate choice known as self-empowerment. In a moment, let's imagine what it may be like to regularly practise self-empowerment. Making self-empowerment a top priority can boost your self-esteem and help you stay motivated to accomplish your goals. You'll trust you have what it takes to overcome challenges and inconveniences so that you won't worry about them. You'll be aware of your advantages and disadvantages and use this knowledge to pursue success on your own terms.

One of the hardest things is feeling like your life is out of control and you're powerless to fix it. Feeling helpless about what's happening can be frustrating. The good news is that you can transform that sensation by mastering self-empowerment.

One of the most crucial things you can do for yourself is to empower yourself. When you're empowered, you can bring about change in your life. You have the option to lead a happy and meaningful life. The moment is for you to take responsibility and control of your life, standing erect, powerful, and exuding the ideal amount of assurance.

Empowering oneself in Islam is fundamentally about realising one's potential, fulfilling responsibilities, and striving for personal and communal growth. This empowerment is not merely about physical or material capabilities but extends to spiritual, intellectual, and moral dimensions. Islam encourages self-empowerment as a means to achieve excellence in faith and contribute positively to society.

One of the key aspects of self-empowerment in Islam is the pursuit of knowledge. The Quran emphasises the importance of seeking knowledge, a path to understanding Allah's (SWT) creation and commandments.

> *Allah (SWT) says in the Quran, "Read in the name of your Lord who created," (Quran 96:1)*

The Prophet Muhammad (PBUH) also emphasised the importance of seeking knowledge and personal development.

> *He said, "Seeking knowledge is an obligation upon every Muslim." (Ibn Majah)*

Moreover, Islam encourages self-empowerment through personal discipline and ethical conduct.

> *The Quran states, "Indeed, Allah (SWT) will not change the condition of a people until they change what is in themselves" (Quran 13:11)*

This verse signifies that personal transformation and empowerment are prerequisites for societal change and improvement. Empowerment also includes being self-reliant and productive.

> *The Prophet Muhammad (PBUH) said, "It is better for one of you to take a rope and cut wood from the forest and carry it on his back and sell it rather than to ask of someone whether he gives him or refuses." (Sahih Bukhari)*

In essence, self-empowerment in Islam is about harnessing one's capabilities to serve Allah (SWT) and humanity, seeking knowledge, maintaining ethical standards, and being proactive and productive. By doing so, Muslims can achieve personal fulfilment and contribute positively to the betterment of society.

Importance of Self-Improvement in Islam

> *The Holy Prophet Muhammad (PBUH) once declared, "Truly, I was sent as a Prophet for the purpose of perfecting human character." (Al-Muwatta)*

This Hadith explains a crucial facet of Islam: the purifying of one's personal attributes as a means of improving oneself. Islam is a way of life that emphasises self-improvement via adherence to the teachings of the Quran and the Prophet Muhammad (PBUH).

Prioritising self-improvement is necessary. Muslims should also strive for a pure intention when on their path of self-improvement and then work towards achieving spiritual purity through tazkiya, or the cleansing of the heart.

> *Allah (SWT) says in the Quran: "Truly Allah (SWT) does not change the condition of a people until they change what is in themselves." (Quran 13:11)*

When Muslims are committed to improving every element of their lives, their good character will shine through to others and enhance society overall. The first step in this dynamic shift is to define and purify one's intention, or niyyah, at the personal level.

> *As the Prophet (PBUH) said: "All actions are judged by their intentions, and each person will be rewarded according to his or her intention." (Sahih Bukhari)*

It is crucial to go out on the path of self-purification with the right intention, aiming to seek Allah's (SWT) pleasure. A Muslim may also be inspired and motivated by the promise of Paradise and an endless, successful existence in the hereafter, bestowed upon those whom Allah (SWT) pleases. When a Muslim lives a life committed to self-improvement in every aspect, their good character will shine through to others.

> *Allah (SWT) says in the Quran: "Allah (SWT) did confer a great favour on the believers when He sent among them an apostle from among themselves, rehearsing unto them the signs of God, sanctifying them, and instructing them in scripture and wisdom, while, before that, they had been in manifest error." (Quran 3:164)*

The process of spiritual purification, known as Tazkiya, or the cleansing of the heart, involves sanctifying or freeing oneself from sin in everything one says and does. Tazkiya calls for the development of mental, emotional, physical, and spiritual discipline. To achieve spiritual health, a Muslim must do various things, such as eating a balanced diet, exercising, controlling their inner dialogue, uttering only moral words, and acting honourably. Muslims are drawn closer to Allah (SWT) when they purify their souls in all respects.

An individual's behaviour is determined by their cardiac condition. A changed heart is always conscious of Allah's (SWT) pleasure and will never act in a way that disobeys His commands. On the other hand, an unclean heart will find it difficult to satisfy Allah (SWT), and even seemingly beneficial deeds could be tarnished by ostentation and bring Him anger. The Prophet (PBUH) highlighted the significance of the heart's condition:

> *"If the heart is sound, the whole body is sound; if corrupt, the body is corrupt" (Sahih Bukhari)*

Tazkiya, or the purification of the heart, is the effort to obey Allah (SWT) and abstain from sin. This includes participating in voluntary worship, carrying out all required deeds, and abstaining from those forbidden. By persevering in this battle, one can become a Muttaqi, an obedient individual cherished by Allah (SWT).

It takes good company to undergo a spiritual transformation. Without a spiritual mentor, one should seek out any pious company to avoid negative influences. However, their advice is vital. Dhikr (remembering Allah SWT) is very important. It begins with vocal recitations and develops into a continuous consciousness of Allah (SWT). Adherence to a disciplined schedule for spiritual exercises guarantees consistent advancement in spiritual correction.

Moreover, Islam holds that spiritual development originates in the heart. Remember that seclusion—withdrawing into solitude for spiritual purification—must be used moderately and as a tool for introspection and introspection. This does not imply or support isolating oneself, as that would be a strategy to avoid fulfilling obligations to the outside world. Helping the less fortunate and treating others with kindness and consideration are essential components of the self-purification regimen. If one lives an ascetic reclusive life, this is not achievable.

Hence, every Muslim should prioritise Tazkiya using the techniques outlined in the Quran and Sunnah. This process will lead to a dedication to serving others altruistically and to Allah's (SWT) satisfaction. An individual who commits their life to the path of self-purification is brimming with goodness. This is the path to prosperity in this life and the next.

> *"By the soul, and the proportion and order given to it, and its inspiration as to its wrong and its right — truly he succeeds who purifies it; and he fails who corrupts it." (Quran 91:7-10)*

Chapter Eight

Strengthening Family and Community Support

Importance of social connections and support networks

In Islam, social connections and support networks are paramount and deeply embedded in the religion's teachings and practices. These connections are not only seen as beneficial for individual well-being but also as a religious obligation that strengthens the Muslim community (ummah).

Everyone needs to interact with others because it's a vital part of life. Each and every individual is dependent on the other to meet their basic requirements. Relationships are built on social interactions, which are how we act and respond to those around us.

Numerous physical and mental advantages stem from positive social contacts, such as enhanced cognitive function, mental well-being, communication abilities, independence, and physical health, particularly for the elderly. Islam promotes contact through the sunnah of

Prophet Muhammad (PBUH) and the numerous revealed verses in the Quran.

It is a religion that strongly emphasises community living and social contact, both supporting the development of brothers and sisters among believers.

> *The Quran teaches, "Indeed, the believers are brothers and sisters, so make peace between your brothers and sisters." (Quran 49:10)*

Prophet Muhammad (PBUH) was renowned for showing mercy and kindness to everyone, regardless of individual differences.

> *He said, "Allah (SWT) is kind, and He loves kindness and confers upon kindness which he does not confer upon severity." (Sahih Muslim)*

Let's have a look at what Islam has instructed us about social connections and support networks.

Building strong family relationships based on Islamic values

Islam values the family highly and views it as the foundation of society. Families are essential for raising morally upright people and pointing them toward righteousness.

A robust and happy family unit is a prerequisite for a thriving and peaceful community. Muslim families are the cornerstone of a community that promotes equity, compassion, and respect for one another.

According to Islamic teachings, it is true that all Muslims believe that Hazrat Adam (AS) and his wife Hazrat Havaa (AS) were the first humans, and it was from them that the rest of humanity derived the concept of family.

> *In the Quran, Allah (SWT) says: "O men, fear your Lord who created you from a single soul, and from it created its match, and spread many men and women from the two. Fear Allah (SWT) in whose name you ask each other (for your rights), and fear (the violation of the rights of) the womb-relations. Surely, Allah (SWT) is watchful over you." (Quran 4:1)*

Islam places a high priority on maintaining family unity. Interestingly, the Arabic word for family, "Usra", is formed from terms that mean unity, cohesion, and protection. Muslims are often reminded, for the same reason, to maintain links within their blood family by the verses of the Quran and the Seerah of our beloved Prophet (PBUH).

The Quran, the holy book of Islam, teaches us the importance of family. A family's ability to grow and thrive depends on developing strong family relationships. For a happy and healthy family atmosphere, it is crucial to forge strong family bonds based on Islamic principles. The importance of family members remaining united and cohesive is emphasised, and it is the duty of parents to establish a setting that encourages respect, love, and harmony within the family.

The first step in establishing strong Islamic family bonds is for parents to provide a good example. Kids pick up life lessons from watching their parents, and kids are more likely to emulate their moral behaviour if parents model it. Establishing a good line of communication is the first step in creating strong family bonds. Regular communication and listening to their wants and concerns are essential for parent-child relationships. A strong link is more likely to exist in a family with effective communication.

Moreover, we ought to be polite and respectful to our family members. A family is made up of people who strongly care for one another and live together. When we take good care of our families, we do what Allah (SWT) desires, contributing to the strength and love of the family unit.

Allah (SWT) commands us to treat our parents with kindness, particularly as they age. They may occasionally irritate us, but it doesn't imply we should treat them badly. Rather, we ought to treat them with kindness and respect. Allah (SWT) states that to show our parents kindness and gratitude for everything they did for us when we were little, we should be humble and pray for them. Thus, by treating our family with love and respect and paying respect to our parents, we make good family members, please Allah (SWT), and improve the community.

> *Prophet Muhammad (PBUH) said: "He who believes in Allah (SWT) and the Last Day, let him maintain good relations with kins." (Sahih Bukhari and Muslim)*

This Hadith clarifies that keeping close relationships is crucial for a sincere believer. Furthermore, the only reason to honour the deed is to please Allah (SWT). A believer experiences Allah's (SWT) kindness and blessings when they surrender their ego.

> *Abu Huraira states, "A man asked the Holy Prophet (PBUH), 'O Muhammad! Who among the people is the most worthy of my good companionship?' The Prophet (PBUH) said, 'Your mother.' The man said, 'Then who?' The Prophet (PBUH) said, 'Then your mother.' The man*

> *further asked, 'Then who?' The Prophet (PBUH) said, 'Then your mother.' The man asked again, 'Then who?' The Prophet (PBUH) said, 'Then your father.'" (Sahih Bukhari and Muslim)*

This Hadith underscores how important it is in Islam to treat one's parents with compassion and companionship, especially the mother. These teachings are in accordance with the Quran's larger message of harmony and togetherness within the family, emphasising the value of upholding strong family ties and treating family members with affection.

In Islam, a healthy relationship with one's siblings is also essential. The Prophet Muhammad (PBUH) instructed Muslims to treat one another as brothers and sisters. This implies that they must not injure one another or allow others to injure them. On the Day of Judgement, Allah (SWT) will reward and assist siblings who assist one another.

Siblings can deepen their relationships and foster a loving family atmosphere by being kind to one another and supporting one another. This cultivates sibling connection and solidarity, reflecting the larger Islamic ideals of compassion and fraternity. Thus, in Islam, a healthy relationship with one's siblings is necessary for both this life and the next.

In addition, the relationship between a husband and wife is also highly important in Islam. Spouses are encouraged to show empathy and understanding for one another to create a caring and encouraging atmosphere. According to the Quran, they should shield and comfort one another, just as they would if they were clothes. Islam believes that to maintain a calm and happy marriage, husband and wife should be patient, kind, and understanding of one another.

Thus, in Islam, maintaining a healthy relationship with your spouse involves more than just being content with one another; it also entails doing what Allah (SWT) commands and strengthening the family.

Throughout his life, Prophet Muhammad (PBUH) provided a wonderful example of a married couple. His marriage to Hazrat Khadijah (RA) is a perfect example of love, adoration, and support. Despite their different ages, they enjoyed a tight friendship based on trust, respect, and understanding. The Prophet Muhammad's (PBUH) closest confidante and ally, Hazrat Khadijah (RA), stood beside him at his darkest moments.

The relationships between Prophet Muhammad (PBUH) and his wives also demonstrate his kindness and consideration for each of them. He would show them affection, participate in deep conversations, and assist with domestic duties. His teachings strongly emphasise the value of showing love and care to one's spouse.

Husbands and wives can forge a solid and loving bond—crucial in Islam—by being kind to one another and cooperating. Their marriage is a source of solace and strength because of this link, which enables them to support one another through good times and bad. Prophet Muhammad (PBUH) set an enduring example for Muslims in their relationships by embodying the ideal of mutual love, respect, and collaboration within marriage.

For believers who devote time and energy to deepening their familial bonds, there are immaterial rewards. Numerous allusions in the Quran and Sunnah encourage us to preserve strong bonds with family members and believe our efforts will be repaid.

> *The Prophet Muhammad (PBUH) said: "Anyone pleased that his sustenance is expanded and his age extended should do kindness to his near relatives." (Sunah Abu Dawud)*

It is said that good deeds strengthen a believer's faith and that treating family members properly and helping them will result in Allah's (SWT) bounties, such as sustenance or Rizq. This may manifest as either provision or health or as both.

Islam emphasises the value of family cohesion and solidarity. It recommends family members support and encourage one another in happy and sad times. This unity creates a sense of security and belonging while fortifying the ties within the family.

Finally, creating strong family relationships with Islamic principles takes constant work and determination. Good values must be ingrained in children by their parents at a young age and reinforced throughout their lives. Although creating a solid family unit is a process that takes time, effort, and sacrifice, the benefits are priceless.

In Islam, the family is a holy institution established by Allah (SWT), not merely a fundamental social unit. Islam strongly emphasises the family as the primary institution for instilling moral principles and values in people. It emphasises affection, kindness, rights, and obligations. Strong familial ties and adherence to Islamic values strengthen the community and foster a culture that values harmony, kindness, and cooperation. As Muslims, we must cherish families and work towards making the world more harmonious.

Fostering community bonds to promote mental well-being

As Muslims, we share our purpose and spirit, bound together by our sense of community. It is possible to find this kind of oneness through participating in various acts of devotion. The relationship strengthens and becomes a powerful support network, adding to the experience. Islamic teachings emphasise the value of community.

As social creatures, we draw energy from positive interactions with others, a blessing from Allah (SWT). We are naturally inclined to look out for one another and improve the lives of those around us.

A fundamental feature of Islam has always been community, even from the time of the Prophet (PBUH) until now. When the Prophet (PBUH) moved from Makkah to Medina, one of his first actions was to construct a masjid to serve as the community's hub. A warm location where people could congregate, exchange knowledge, tell tales, and perform acts of worship in unison—all for the sake of Allah (SWT). Making connections and being kind to one another is a crucial component of our faith, permeating all our rituals, ideals, and daily activities.

> *Holy Prophet (PBUH) said: "The believers in their mutual kindness, compassion and sympathy are just like one body. When one of the limbs suffers, the whole body responds to it with wakefulness and fever." (Sahih Bukhari and Muslim)*

Within the intricate web of Islamic beliefs, brotherhood is deeply ingrained and highly valued. Islam's definition of brotherhood goes beyond simple blood ties to include the spiritual ties that bind Muslim communities around the world. Islam's concept of brotherhood, known as "Ukhuwah," is firmly embedded in its central tenets. It represents a link of cooperation and support between Muslims. The Quran stresses the importance of nurturing this special bond among believers.

> *Allah (SWT) says: "The believers are but brothers, so make settlement between your brothers. And fear Allah (SWT) that you may receive mercy." (Quran 49:10)*

This verse emphasises the significance of maintaining the spirit of brotherhood and finding peaceful solutions to promote the unity of believers.

> *Allah (SWT) says: "The believing men and believing women are allies of one another. They enjoin what is right and forbid what is wrong." (Quran 9:71)*

This verse highlights the cooperation and support Muslims should provide for one another.

In Islam, brotherhood is a manner of life that promotes harmony, kindness, and solidarity among Muslims rather than just a theoretical idea. By upholding the ideals of brotherhood, Muslims can deepen their faith and build a more peaceful, compassionate community. As Muslims, we are responsible for assisting and supporting our brothers and sisters in need everywhere and fostering brotherhood within our own communities.

In addition, belonging to a community greatly benefits a person's physical, emotional, and mental wellness. Islam views the community as more than just getting together; it also refers to coming together for spiritual growth, mutual support, and worship.

Let's examine the significance of community involvement in Islam.

For example, when you study the Quran together as a society, you take part in an enlightenment journey alongside your fellow humans. Every passage is considered; you assist those falling behind and uplift Muslims who struggle with reading, all while gathering blessings from Allah (SWT). A sense of support and community from this journey is invaluable for keeping one's motivation high while studying the Quran.

> *In the Quran, Allah (SWT) highlights the significance of community: "And hold firmly to the rope of Allah (SWT) all together and do not become divided..." (Quran 3:103)*

It can be intimidating to memorise and recite the entire Quran by yourself. However, you may simply traverse the murky seas with the support of your community. Your community will turn into a network of support that will help you get through it by providing direction and inspiration. As a community is made up of individuals with a range of perspectives, you will have access to a variety of insights. Select the ones that suit you the most, and make thoughtful enquiries that will advance your education.

The community call of the Quran is aptly reminded when the Quran is recited in a group setting. Every verse that is recited enhances societal cohesion and individual faith. Your Quranic journey will be aided by the motivating and uplifting influence of learning together.

Today, loneliness is a plague that spreads quickly across homes. It alters perspective and raises stress levels, impacting general health and well-being. It's so simple to get estranged from everyone, yet the strength of an Islamic community can bring you back to life.

Being a part of a community implies that you have individuals who will ask how you're doing even when you're not feeling well. These folks will offer you their prayers and wholehearted support. Communities aid in removing feelings of isolation and providing a sense of acceptance.

It might be challenging to stay engaged with your Quran in a world full of distractions. However, your communities have the power to instil in you the everyday practice of remembering Allah (SWT).

Attending social events centred on Islamic studies will help you remember and stay on the right track. With this, you can imitate the Prophets and incorporate the lessons of the Quran into your everyday life with ease.

Islam encourages communal responsibility among its members. Muslims are encouraged to actively contribute to the well-being of their fellow humans; therefore, the idea of shared responsibility will aid in developing this virtue while you live in a community. It will teach you to accept responsibility and improve you as a person.

Islam promotes cooperation across various Islamic organisations. Islamic centres and mosques may coexist, and you'll get to widen your support system. You can establish relationships and help others with ease. These networks can provide social interaction, mentoring, and knowledge-sharing possibilities. They are crucial in offering a framework for people who are in need of assistance or are going through difficult times.

Islam, in its simplest form, urges its adherents to uphold their interpersonal ties with other Muslims as well as their personal relationship with Allah (SWT). It is your duty as a Muslim to participate in your community.

Role of empathy, compassion, and mutual assistance in Islam

The notion of solidarity, understanding, and support among Muslims is emphasised by the statement, *"The believers in their mutual compassion, kindness, and empathy are just like one body."* The following instances from Islamic history and the life of the Prophet Muhammad (PBUH) demonstrate this idea:

Assistance to the Needy: The Holy Prophet (PBUH) stressed the value of helping those in need. He encouraged Muslims to aid the least disadvantaged and donate to charity. Because of this culture of compassion and goodwill, institutions like Sadaqah (voluntary charity) and Zakat (obligatory almsgiving) were established.

Sharing Happiness and Sadness: The Prophet (PBUH) and his companions would experience happiness and sadness together when a believer did. The ties of unity and fraternity were strengthened by this activity.

Praying for One Another: The Prophet (PBUH) urged followers to pray for one another's health. This practice embodies the spirit of the Hadith, which is about Muslims being like one body, encouraging compassion and care for one another.

Distribution of Wealth: There have been stories of believers helping one another by pooling their riches during the Prophet's (PBUH) lifetime. The migrants from Makkah who were forced to flee their homes were graciously received and supported by the people of Medina. A strong community was aided in its development by this sense of solidarity.

Reconciliation: The Prophet (PBUH) made a concerted effort to mediate disagreements among his friends. He instilled in them the value of settling disputes amicably and preserving solid bonds between people to preserve the idea of kindness and sympathy for one another.

Mutual Assistance: One of the best examples of mutual support and assistance is the early Muslim community in Medina. Whether amid a famine or a war, they cooperated when things became tough. One instance of Muslim assistance for one another in combat is the Battle of Uhud.

Visiting the Sick: The Holy Prophet (PBUH) stressed the need to visit sick people. This kind of kindness not only demonstrates empathy and compassion but also serves as more evidence of the notion that the community is a unit and that members should help one another in times of need.

The values of empathy, compassion, and mutual assistance are deeply embedded in Islam, shaping a community that thrives on solidarity and support. The Prophet Muhammad (PBUH) exemplified and instilled these virtues through various teachings and practices. Ultimately, Islam fosters a sense of unity and collective well-being, reinforcing the belief that the community, like one body, must work together with empathy and compassion to ensure the welfare of all its members.

Chapter Nine

Addressing Trauma and Grief

Healing from trauma through Islamic principles

Muslims deal with serious problems and crises all around the world, which can have a negative effect on their mental health. These difficulties include trauma and the consequences of Islamophobia, especially in countries where Muslims are socially marginalised.

Overcoming cultural and religious barriers, the quest for trauma healing is an international endeavour. Islam's teachings and tenets provide a special framework for dealing with and overcoming trauma. Let's investigate how Islamic guidance can offer comfort, empowerment, healing from trauma, and a route back to emotional and spiritual wholeness.

Coping with trauma and hardship in accordance with Sunnah practices

Extremely stressful experiences that break your sense of security and leave you feeling helpless in a frightening environment can cause emotional and psychological trauma. You may struggle with persistently uncomfortable memories, feelings, and anxiety as a result of psychological trauma. It may lead to a sense of numbness, disconnection, and a loss of trust in others.

The Prophet's (PBUH) answer to great adversity was to turn to Allah (SWT). When the Prophet (PBUH) faced difficulties, he followed these two steps:

- **Pray to Allah (SWT) and put his trust in Him**

One of the main tenets of Islamic practice is prayer, or Salah, which can effectively treat trauma. Prayer regularly provides times of comfort, reflection, and intimacy with Allah (SWT).

People who turn to prayer might take solace in knowing Allah (SWT) is ever-present and aware of their difficulties. Furthermore, making duas, or supplications, can be a way to communicate one's emotions and ask for divine support in overcoming trauma.

- **Consult with his reliable confidantes for advice**

Getting professional help is not just acceptable but highly recommended. Islam emphasises self-care and overall well-being heavily. Seeking advice from mental health specialists, therapists, or counsellors with training in trauma treatment is consistent with Islamic principles that place a high value on recovery and self-improvement.

The Holy Prophet's (PBUH) life is a roadmap for dealing with loss and mourning. The Prophet's (PBUH) life exemplified tenacity and divine submission, inspiring believers.

Grief can all result in resilience, understanding, and greater spiritual connections. Islam combines practical actions, group support, and spiritual guidance to promote healing and strength.

Even when the Prophet's (PBUH) eyes and heart were bleeding, he did not doubt Allah (SWT) or disrespect Him with his lips. That is the essence of the issue and the advice found in Islam for coping with loss and trauma.

While the Prophet (PBUH) did not repress his feelings, he refused to let them dictate his views or behaviour. The Prophet (PBUH) did not hesitate to seek advice from others and confided in his loved ones, yet he understood that Allah (SWT) was ultimately his saviour.

Within the context of Islam, trauma healing is a complex process having psychological, emotional, and spiritual components. By applying the lessons in the Quran and the guidance provided by Prophet Muhammad (PBUH), people can find comfort, empowerment, and support while they work towards healing.

Through obtaining expert aid, strengthening one's relationship with Allah (SWT), reflecting and being thankful, looking for community support, doing good deeds, and accepting forgiveness, people can start a life-changing healing path that unites faith and well-being.

Managing Trauma the Islamic Way

The world serves as a testing ground for Allah's (SWT) slaves. It is a location where it will be decided if the individual will succeed and be allowed entry into heaven or the opposite. The exam to measure our tolerance, compliance, and appreciation might take many different shapes.

It may manifest as a kind of hunger, trauma, terror, or the loss of something or someone. Having children and being wealthy are two things that will put people to the test in this world.

Every believer will face difficulties throughout their lives, and success will only come after each trial. Each person will face an examination depending on their aptitude and level of faith. Islam teaches a variety of techniques for handling trauma, such as:

Following the Sunnah of Prophet Muhammad (PBUH) and adhering to Allah's (SWT) instruction are two methods of spiritual intervention. Allah (SWT) has guaranteed that people who abide by these will live peacefully.

A traumatised individual should fervently and consistently seek Allah's (SWT) assistance. Allah (SWT) will make it easier for the person to overcome the obstacle and the weight they carry.

A person who submits to the Creator of this universe and puts their trust in Allah (SWT) is one who remembers Allah (SWT). A traumatised individual ought to offer numerous dua and Dhikr.

All that occurs to us results from Allah's (SWT) will. It was predetermined for 50,000 years before the formation of the earth and heavens. It was always going to happen this way. Keeping this belief in mind will be easier and quicker for an individual to recover.

For someone to heal from trauma, social support is also crucial. We call it collectivism. Helping the traumatised individual adjust to reality is the coping strategy used in social assistance. Good social support plays a beneficial role in keeping someone from experiencing psychological trauma.

Managing trauma in the Islamic way combines spiritual and social approaches for holistic healing. Islam views the world as a testing ground, with trials like trauma being part of divine assessment. Individuals find peace and strength by following the Sunnah of Prophet Muhammad (PBUH) and adhering to Allah's (SWT) guidance.

Seeking Allah's (SWT) help through prayers (dua) and remembrance (Dhikr) fosters trust in the divine plan. Accepting that all events are preordained by Allah (SWT) provides comfort.

Social support, or collectivism, is crucial, offering communal care that aids in coping and adjustment, highlighting the importance of unity and empathy in healing.

Incorporating therapeutic techniques grounded in Islamic values

Therapy is the process of addressing dysfunctional behaviours, beliefs, and interpersonal problems. During treatment, the client discusses their issues from their perspective. For therapy to be effective, the counsellor or therapist must understand the client's culture, way of life, and religious convictions.

Mental health therapists must honour their clients' cultural and religious beliefs and provide them with appropriate support. Nonetheless, a lot of individuals who require mental health assistance choose not to receive clinical counselling or therapy. There are several reasons why people reject treatment, one of which is the concern that it will harm their religious beliefs.

Our way of living as Muslims is dictated by our faith in Islam. As a result, our healing process is closely tied to our Islamic values and teachings. A Muslim counsellor may use passages from the Quran or Hadiths from the Prophet (PBUH) to help us heal since they know our worldview and the significance of the Quran and the Sunnah for our well-being. As previously noted, fasting, supplication, and prayer are therapeutic practices in Islam. For example, fasting has been demonstrated to be good for our physical health.

Fasting improves our mental and physical health by sharpening our focus and allowing us time to reflect on the gifts we have received from Allah (SWT). The demand for Muslim counsellors is rising within the Muslim community, as Islamic counselling plays a crucial role in guiding Muslim clients on their path to recovery. Fortunately, there are plenty of Muslim counsellors who work with a range of age groups and specialise in different aspects of mental health.

Integrating therapeutic techniques grounded in Islamic values to treat trauma and grief involves a holistic approach that combines psychological methods with spiritual and religious principles. Here are some strategies to consider:

- **Islamic Cognitive Behavioral Therapy (ICBT)**

Evidence-based treatments such as Cognitive Behavioural Therapy (CBT) have shown promise in treating a variety of mental health conditions. CBT gives people the tools they need to create positive changes in their lives by assisting them in understanding their thoughts, feelings, and behaviours through a cooperative and controlled approach.

Individuals can learn to replace negative thought patterns with more accurate and beneficial ones by recognising and confronting them. Through this process, one can become more self-aware and learn effective coping mechanisms.

It motivates individuals to participate in pursuits that enhance their well-being and mental health. Cognitive behavioural therapy (CBT) is a comprehensive therapeutic technique that addresses behavioural and cognitive elements.

Example: Utilising verses from the Quran and Hadith to reinforce positive thinking and behaviours. For instance, reflecting on Surah Ash-Sharh (The Relief) reminds individuals that with hardship comes ease.

- **Ruqyah (Spiritual Healing)**

Ruqyah is sometimes misinterpreted by Muslims as a way to speak with bad spirits. In actuality, this is untrue. The practice of Ruqyah bears similarities to dua in that it involves the recital of certain verses from the Quran along with various incantations and invocations based on the Prophetic tradition. These lines in Ruqyah are all essentially begging Allah (SWT) to increase our Iman and be our sanctuary.

Though the term "Ruqyah" is not explicitly mentioned in the Quran or the Sunnah, there are indications in multiple verses and Prophetic traditions that Ruqyah dua and other Quranic verses can heal human diseases and provide Muslims who practise it with a sense of peace and tranquillity. Therefore, Muslims should understand the significance of the following Ruqyah passages for the soul and body to experience both spiritual and bodily solace:

> *"And say, "Truth has come, and falsehood has vanished. Falsehood is surely bound to vanish." And We send down in the Quran that which is a cure and a mercy for the believers." (Quran 17:81-2)*

Ruqyah is a way for all Muslims to strengthen their Iman and relationship with Allah (SWT). Here are three key considerations to keep in mind before beginning any Ruqyah practice to ensure you start on the right path.

Purpose

The slightest intention underlies every action. It can just be a passing idea or a well-considered goal. As soon as you start the Ruqyah treatment, make amends with Allah (SWT) and ask Him to keep you safe and to drive out all evil through the words of the Quran.

Conviction

It is not desirable to repeat Ruqyah verses without understanding their significance. When performing Ruqya on yourself, you must do so with complete assurance, repeating the verses of the Quran aloud and clearly and believing that Allah (SWT) is the only One who can grant the Cure.

Consistency and Patience

You shouldn't treat Ruqyah as a one-time thing or take it for granted. Insha'Allah, you have to do it continuously to eventually gain from it. It could take days, months, or even years for some people. Every day, recite the Ruqyah verses and dua. Big things happen to people who endure and wait patiently.

Example: Using Surah Al-Fatiha, Ayat-ul-Kursi, and the last two verses of Surah Al-Baqarah for their protective and soothing effects.

- **Fasting (Sawm) and Spiritual Reflection**

Fasting, particularly during Ramadan, is a time for spiritual reflection and increased worship. Fasting can help individuals develop self-discipline, empathy for others, and a deeper connection with their faith.

Example: Observing voluntary fasts outside of Ramadan and using the time for prayer and introspection.

- **Gratitude Practice (Shukr)**

Practising gratitude is a key aspect of Islamic teachings. Encouraging individuals to focus on the blessings in their lives and express gratitude to Allah (SWT).

Example: Keeping a gratitude journal, where you list daily things for which you are thankful, shifts your focus from the negative to the positive aspects of life.

By combining these therapeutic techniques with professional mental health support, individuals can find a balanced and effective way to heal from trauma and grief while staying true to their Islamic values.

Encouraging emotional healing through forgiveness and acceptance

Forgiveness is a powerful tool in a society where suffering and hurt are commonplace. This idea is ingrained in the fabric of our existence as humans, irrespective of our backgrounds or beliefs. True healing and magic can happen when you forgive, regardless of whether you give yourself to Allah (SWT), the universe, or another revered higher force.

Letting go of grudges that hold us connected to the wrongs done to us is a necessary part of forgiveness. It involves letting go of hurt, anger, or pointless ruminating so that we don't waste too much mental or emotional energy on them and continue with our lives.

Holding a grudge is like ingesting poison and praying it affects the other person. It is similar to bearing a tremendous load of animosity and hatred. Grudges are problematic because, aside from being awkward to carry around, they accomplish none of the intended aims. They don't mend our wounds or make us feel better.

Ultimately, we become attached to our resentments, holding onto them as if they were valuable possessions. Yet, they continue to deprive us of the comfort we've long desired since the initial injury. To remind ourselves and others of our suffering and deservingness, we transform our resentment into an object we hold at arm's length.

In actuality, whereas our resentment stems from our suffering, it is not tied to our hearts; rather, it is a mental construct that tells the tale of what occurred to us. True healing is impeded when our resentment turns into a boulder that keeps the light of love from entering our hearts. Unfortunately, the empathy our grudge seeks to evoke ultimately fails to provide, leaving us unable to let go of it. Thus, shifting your viewpoint can truly help you get things right.

Forgiveness takes time; it's a process of development and reconciliation. Through introspection, developing empathy, and learning to let go, we can move compassionately and purposefully through the forgiveness landscape. By adopting these doable actions, we may rewrite our emotional histories and mend wounds that have festered for far too long.

Self-examination serves as a beacon for those who choose to forgive. It involves looking inward to comprehend our own emotions and driving forces. Through introspection, we may find the causes of our emotions, recognise our triggers, and peel back the layers of hurt.

While it doesn't excuse the wrongs done to us, developing empathy makes the offender more human. It enables us to recognise that, just like us, they are flawed humans figuring out the complexities of life. Empathy weakens the barriers of animosity, opening the door to forgiveness.

It takes patience and practice to become skilled at letting go. To forgive, we must let go of our grudges; to achieve that, we need useful tools. By keeping a journal, we create a space to express our feelings and release them from the constraints of our thoughts. Practising mindfulness lets us watch our emotions without judgment and let them come and go.

In conclusion, forgiveness is a journey that leads to emotional freedom and healing. By letting go of grudges, embracing empathy, and practising self-examination and mindfulness, we can foster a heart open to love and compassion. This path not only heals our own wounds but also contributes to a more understanding and harmonious world.

Chapter Ten

Balancing Mental Health and Spiritual Growth

Integrating mental health care with spirituality

Integrating mental health care with spiritual development offers a holistic approach to well-being that acknowledges the interconnectedness of the mind, body, and spirit. Mental health care addresses psychological, emotional, and social issues through therapies, counselling, and medication.

On the other hand, spiritual development seeks meaning, purpose, and connection beyond oneself, often through religious practices, meditation, mindfulness, and philosophical inquiry. By merging these two aspects, individuals can receive comprehensive care that addresses all facets of their being.

Embracing a holistic approach to well-being in Islam

Embracing a holistic approach to well-being in Islam involves integrating spiritual, mental, and physical health practices to achieve a balanced and fulfilling life. Islam, as a comprehensive way of life,

KEEPING SABR

offers guidance on nurturing each aspect of an individual's well-being, emphasising the interconnectedness of the mind, body, and soul.

The Quran contains verses emphasising the need to sustain well-being in all facets of life, acknowledging the delicate balance that exists between the mind and body.

> *Allah (SWT) says in the Quran: "And do not throw yourselves into destruction." (Quran 2:195)*

The need to maintain our well-being and practise self-care is emphasised in the above verse.

The teachings of the Holy Quran and Islam offer guidance that benefits everyone, touching on all aspects of life, including mental well-being. The following are some pearls of Islamic wisdom that, if taken in their truest sense, may help us comprehend mental health concerns by providing a fresh perspective.

We rely on Allah (SWT) for all of our bodily, mental, and spiritual well-being because we sincerely believe that He is the ultimate and real Healer, Al-Shafi.

- **Hope sustains us**

Because hope makes it possible for us to see the light in the midst of all the darkness, it may work miracles when it comes to mental health issues or any other heavy load or struggle.

It is especially important for those who are already depressed because hopelessness makes people withdraw from life, avoid activities they normally like, or spend less time with loved ones.

The Holy Quran has a powerful message of hope that Allah (SWT) has imparted.

> "Say, 'O My servants who have committed excesses against their own souls! despair not of the mercy of Allah (SWT), surely Allah (SWT) forgives all sins.'" (Quran 39:54)

Allah (SWT) assures us that we can make amends in the present for any faults we may have done in the past. Dwelling on the past won't do us any good while doing nothing to right the wrong.

- **Life's meaning and purpose**

Islam aims to set people free from the bonds of this world by submitting them to Allah (SWT). It tells us that acknowledging Allah (SWT) as our Creator and committing to His precepts is the first step towards our deliverance and salvation. Pursuing Allah (SWT) is more important than anything else, even if humans can have fun, amuse themselves, and accomplish their worldly objectives within Allah's (SWT) bounds. It offers a unique reason for existing.

- **After adversity, ease is promised**

The universal reality that there are times of ease and hardship in life is another encouraging message for anyone who is experiencing depression or low mood. This is found in the Holy Quran. Allah (SWT) has promised relief from every adversity. The Holy Quran instructs us to persevere through adversity and times of suffering with fortitude and bravery and never give up. The Holy Prophet Muhammad's (PBUH) teachings state that if we patiently endure hardship and do not give up on Allah (SWT), we will be rewarded with eternal life or the afterlife.

- **Trust in Allah's (SWT) plan**

Islam instils perseverance and faith in Allah's (SWT) purpose. The Quran tells us that hardships are a natural part of life and that developing patience in the face of difficulties can help one become resilient and have inner strength. Even during challenging times, we can feel at peace with faith in Allah's (SWT) knowledge and purpose.

- **Self-care as a practical spirituality**

Self-care is not just regarded as a contemporary habit in Islam but also as a spiritual obligation. Taking care of the body and the soul, the Prophet Muhammad (PBUH) advocated for seeking balance in all aspects of life.

> *The Quran echoes this idea when it says, "And He found you lost and guided [you]." (Quran 93:7)*

This verse exhorts us to use introspection and self-care to seek direction. It highlights that honouring the life the Creator gave us begins with caring for ourselves. We are urged to take proactive measures to attain mental and emotional wellness, just as Allah (SWT) leads the loss. It all comes down to realising that caring for our health is a spiritual duty.

- **The holistic method**

As stated in the Quran (29:45), prayer is a way to find serenity in the midst of life's difficulties and a way to express worship. It provides comfort and stability by bringing our hearts and minds into harmony with heavenly tranquillity. Prayer can help us centre ourselves when stress strikes, offering a deep sense of resilience and serenity.

In addition to directing our devotion, the wisdom of the Quran and Hadith helps us achieve holistic well-being, which entails treating our mental health with the same consideration and deliberate effort as our spiritual and physical well-being. Essentially, our faith provides a wealth of knowledge on mental health, including ideas that both Muslims can find helpful in compassionately preserving mental health.

Avoiding spiritual bypassing and embracing emotional authenticity

Avoiding spiritual bypassing and embracing emotional authenticity in Islam involves acknowledging and addressing emotional challenges directly rather than using spiritual practices to avoid or suppress them. Spiritual bypassing occurs when individuals use religious or spiritual beliefs to avoid dealing with painful feelings, unresolved wounds, or psychological issues.

In Islam, emotional authenticity is rooted in the understanding that human emotions are a natural part of life. The Quran and Hadith emphasise the importance of acknowledging and expressing emotions appropriately. Prophet Muhammad (PBUH) experienced and expressed a wide range of emotions, including grief, joy, and anger, demonstrating that it is natural and acceptable to feel and express emotions.

To avoid spiritual bypassing, it is crucial to integrate spiritual practices with genuine emotional work. This means using prayer, meditation, and other spiritual activities as tools for deeper self-awareness and healing rather than escaping emotional pain. For instance, during Salah (prayer), one can reflect on their feelings and seek guidance from Allah (SWT) on how to address them constructively.

Embracing emotional authenticity involves being honest with oneself and others about one's feelings. This includes seeking help through counselling, support groups, or trusted community members. Islam encourages seeking knowledge and assistance in all areas of life, including mental health.

> *The Prophet (PBUH) said, "The strong person is not the one who can overpower others, but the one who can control themselves in the face of anger." (Ahmad)*

Furthermore, practising self-compassion and understanding is vital. Islam teaches the importance of mercy and compassion, both towards others and oneself. Treating oneself with kindness and understanding rather than judgment can facilitate healing and personal growth when facing emotional difficulties.

Avoiding spiritual bypassing and embracing emotional authenticity in Islam involves integrating spiritual practices. This approach ensures a balanced and authentic engagement with spiritual and emotional aspects of life, leading to holistic well-being and personal growth.

Emphasising the importance of self-awareness and self-care in spiritual practices

Emphasising the importance of self-awareness and self-care in spiritual practices is essential for holistic well-being. People with this self-awareness capacity can overcome their shortcomings and enjoy spiritually satisfying lives. As Muslims, we believe introspection and self-improvement are essential to our faith.

In actuality, Islam declared more than 1400 years ago that the greatest jihad is the quest for self-reformation. Numerous verses in the Holy Quran exhort believers to "ponder" and "reflect." Psychology is just now beginning to recognise the advantages of self-awareness.

Understanding oneself results in understanding Allah (SWT). How, though, are these two categories of knowledge related? By studying ourselves, our capacities, how our bodies work, and how we are shaped and designed, we can refocus on the existence of an ultimate Creator—the Fashioner and the Giver of Life, Allah (SWT).

Accepting our frailties helps us see how dependent we must be on The Most Powerful Allah (SWT). Knowing our shortcomings allows us to improve them, bringing us closer to Allah (SWT) and keeping us from committing sins. Similarly, by being conscious of our strengths, we can make the most of them and apply them to improve our environment, relationships with others, and proximity to Allah (SWT) and His pleasure.

It becomes increasingly clear as we have a deeper understanding of our shortcomings and abilities that we have nothing to do with our development. Every indication that we are surrounded by or part of a higher, supreme entity whose existence cannot be denied leads us back to this ultimate being. Being more conscious allows us to maintain emotional self-control.

Everybody thinks. Humans possess the ability to reflect on and assess various situations. However, self-awareness enables us to keep an eye on our thoughts, which provides us with an understanding of our goals and motivations. For instance, every idea that arises in our minds has a source.

Most of the time, we are preoccupied with thoughts about our everyday routines or relationships with others. We brood about rudeness all day long when it happens at work. It's so easy for our minds to take over and our ideas to become negative.

Self-awareness interrupts that pattern of behaviour. We can sincerely repent and grow if we become aware of our ideas and unfavourable feelings. This can help us purify ourselves and receive Allah's (SWT) genuine benefits.

In Islam, self-awareness through regular self-reflection (Muhasabah) helps Muslims evaluate actions and intentions, strengthening their relationship with Allah (SWT). As emphasised in the Quran and Hadith, self-care includes maintaining health through proper nutrition, exercise, and rest.

This balanced approach prevents burnout, promotes genuine healing, aligns actions with spiritual goals, and enhances overall well-being and fulfilment.

Chapter Eleven

Seeking Professional Help and Guidance

Importance of professional mental health support in Islam

Islam places a strong emphasis on maintaining one's health by refusing to stigmatise others, obtaining medical attention from a professional when necessary, and facing disease with patience and prayer. It is cultural attitudes, not religious teachings, that are primarily responsible for stigmatised views on mental illness. Mental health problems are not to be disregarded or stigmatised. Islam understands the importance of getting expert assistance when necessary.

> *The Prophet Muhammad (PBUH) said, "Seeking medical treatment is obligatory." (Ibn Majah)*

This Hadith highlights how crucial it is to have professional assistance, especially psychological assistance, to get the proper care. Islam promotes asking for assistance from both professional and spiritual sources. Anxiety may worsen if mental health issues are not recognised and treated. Islam encourages people to overcome personal issues by seeking advice from mental health specialists or religious leaders. Let's have a look at this!

Removing the stigma associated with seeking counselling and therapy

A significant obstacle for those who have a mental illness is still the stigma associated with mental illness. Even if the state of mental health care has greatly improved in recent years, many people still decide not to get treatment or end it too soon. Stigma is one of the many potential causes of these differences, albeit arguably the most important.

When someone perceives you negatively due to a distinguishing feature or personal attribute that is perceived as, or is, a disadvantage, it is known as stigma (a negative stereotype). Regrettably, stigmatising attitudes and ideas about individuals with mental health disorders are widespread.

Discrimination may result from stigma. Discrimination can be overt and straightforward, like when someone remarks negatively about your mental health condition or the way you're being treated. Alternatively, it could be inadvertent or subtly expressed, such as when someone avoids you because they believe you might be violent, unpredictable, or dangerous because of your mental condition. You might even be critical of yourself.

Social stigma persists even among Muslims who have positive views towards mental health treatment. Disclosure of mental illness is deemed "shameful" due to concerns about family social standing. Stigma causes inequities and even disastrous outcomes for people with mental illnesses as well as their communities.

People may decide not to associate with mental health clinics or experts to avoid being labelled as psychiatric patients; this way, they can escape being diagnosed by not seeking mental health care.

Overall, stigma creates substantial barriers, causing people to avoid mental health services and perpetuating negative outcomes for both individuals and communities. Addressing and removing this stigma is essential for encouraging more people to seek counselling and therapy, ultimately improving mental health care accessibility and effectiveness.

Strategies for overcoming stigma

Receive medical treatment. It might be hard for you to acknowledge that you need help. Don't let the stigma associated with mental illness keep you from getting the care you need. Treatment can bring relief by determining the underlying causes of your issues and reducing symptoms that interfere with your personal and professional life.

Avoid letting stigma foster guilt and self-doubt. Remember, social stigma is not limited to other people. You may think your illness is a reflection of your weakness or that you should be able to handle it alone. Building self-esteem and overcoming harmful self-judgment can be achieved by seeking counselling, learning more about your illness, and connecting with others who also struggle with mental illness.

Participate in a support group. Certain national and local organisations provide internet resources and local programmes to educate the public, families, and individuals with mental illness, therefore lowering stigma try to connect with them.

Advocate against stigma. Think about sharing your thoughts online, in letters to the editor, or at events. It can raise awareness of mental illness among the general population and inspire courage in those suffering comparable difficulties. People's opinions are usually the result of ignorance rather than information derived from facts. Learning to accept your illness and understand what you need to do to treat it, as well as seeking assistance and educating others, can make a great difference.

To overcome the stigma surrounding mental health, focus on increasing awareness through education by highlighting that mental health conditions are common and treatable. Promote open conversations to normalise discussions and share personal experiences to build empathy.

Challenge negative stereotypes by presenting accurate information and advocating for mental health representation in media.

Finally, seek support from mental health professionals and communities to foster a culture of acceptance and understanding.

Resources for accessing mental health services within the Muslim community

Accessing mental health services within the Muslim community can involve several approaches, both locally and online.

Here are some resources and strategies for promoting mental health education and advocacy:

Local Resources

Islamic Centres and Mosques:

Many Islamic centres and mosques offer counselling services or partner with mental health professionals. They might also host workshops and lectures on mental health topics.

Muslim Mental Health Professionals:

Look for directories of Muslim therapists, counsellors, and psychologists. Organisations such as the Muslim Mental Health Network can help find professionals who understand Islamic perspectives on mental health.

Community Organisations:

Local Muslim community organisations often offer support groups, mental health workshops, and educational events. They may also provide resources for finding culturally competent mental health professionals.

Online Resources

Muslim Mental Health Organisations:

Muslim Mental Health Foundation: Provides information on mental health resources and advocates for better mental health services within the Muslim community.

National Alliance on Mental Illness (NAMI): Offers resources on mental health, including support for various communities.

Online Counselling Platforms:

Websites like BetterHelp and Talkspace offer online counselling services. Look for therapists with experience in Islamic mental health issues or who are open to understanding Islamic values.

Social Media:

Follow mental health advocates and organisations on platforms like Instagram and Twitter. Accounts focusing on mental health within the Muslim community can provide useful tips and resources.

Promoting Mental Health Education and Advocacy

To promote mental health education within the Muslim community, several strategies can be implemented. Organising or attending workshops that address mental health topics from an Islamic perspective can be particularly effective in dispelling myths and educating community members about the importance of mental health.

Collaborating with Islamic institutions, such as mosques, Islamic schools, and community centres, to integrate mental health education into their programmes can further strengthen these efforts.

Utilising media and publications by writing articles, creating videos, or starting a podcast focused on mental health issues within the community offers a platform to share stories and advice that resonate with the audience.

Establishing or participating in support groups and peer networks provides a safe space for discussing mental health challenges and sharing coping strategies.

Additionally, launching advocacy and awareness campaigns can help raise awareness about mental health issues and reduce stigma by highlighting personal stories and successful case studies that illustrate the benefits of seeking help. By leveraging these resources and strategies, valuable support and education can be provided to the Muslim community.

Chapter Twelve

Conclusion

By exploring the Sunnah's rich guidance on managing emotions, stress, and adversity, this book underscores the holistic approach Islam offers for nurturing emotional and mental well-being. The practices discussed—ranging from spiritual healing and resilience building to seeking professional help—demonstrates the comprehensive nature of Islamic support for mental health.

Our journey through the chapters has highlighted the significance of integrating spiritual principles with practical strategies to foster a balanced and fulfilling life. By embracing the wisdom of the Prophet Muhammad (PBUH) and recognising the importance of community and professional support, individuals can find a pathway to healing and strength.

It is our hope that the insights and practices shared in this book serve as a beacon of support for those navigating the challenges of mental health, empowering them to cultivate serenity, resilience, and a deeper connection with their faith. May these teachings guide and inspire readers toward a more harmonious and resilient life.

Find Out More

Website: www.barakahinbusiness.com

Socials: @barakahinbusiness

If you enjoyed this book, kindly leave a review to help expand our reach so others may benefit also.

www.ingramcontent.com/pod-product-compliance
Lightning Source LLC
Chambersburg PA
CBHW050208130526
44590CB00043B/3237